NO CRYING
IN THE OPERATING ROOM

NO CRYING

IN THE OPERATING ROOM

My Life as an International Relief Doctor, from Haiti,
to South Sudan, to the Syrian Civil War

A Memoir

CECILY WANG, M.D.

gatekeeper press™
Tampa, Florida

The views and opinions expressed in this book are solely those of the author and do not reflect the views or opinions of Gatekeeper Press. Gatekeeper Press is not to be held responsible for and expressly disclaims responsibility for the content herein.

No Crying in the Operating Room: My Life as an International Relief Doctor, from Haiti, to South Sudan, to the Syrian Civil War A Memoir

Published by Gatekeeper Press
7853 Gunn Hwy, Suite 209
Tampa, FL 33626
www.GatekeeperPress.com

Library of Congress Control Number: 2023935406

ISBN (hardcover): 9781662936845
ISBN (paperback): 9781662936852
eISBN: 9781662936869

Table of Contents

Note: Some names and identifying details have been changed.

Introduction

I'm a trauma surgeon and an ICU doctor based in Hawaii. I've also spent the last decade working as a doctor on international medical missions, with Médecins Sans Frontières (Doctors Without Borders) and other relief groups. I wrote this book to share how my views on medicine have changed as a result of my experience on these missions.

In medical school and residency, I became disillusioned by how regulations and the bottom line compromised the care we offer patients. On international medical relief trips I have found medical practice as it should be, with the patient's health all that matters. This is not to say that there are not extensive problems with how international medical aid is conducted, but somewhere along the way I have rediscovered the idealism that first encouraged me to become a doctor.

I also wrote this book to try and capture how I've been changed by my experiences in witnessing both the best and the worst of what humanity has to offer. When we're willing to be changed by our experiences, we open ourselves to becoming better humans.

For those considering a career in medicine, I offer these simple lessons learned: maintain a balance between emotional control and compassion in the operating room and ICU. Even if you believe you have made no mistakes, it's an important practice to review your work at the end of each shift. The key to success lies in the details; make sure to focus on doing the basics well.

Cecily Wang, M.D.
Honolulu, Hawaii
May 1, 2023

To Rocky and Kayla

I'm so grateful to have you in my life.

Rocky, you make the world a better place
and I'm incredibly lucky to be your sister.

Kayla, you amaze me every day and I'm proud of you.
Thank you for always thinking of everything and everyone.

I love you both very much.

Chapter One
Haiti Changed Everything

The houses swept past, ramshackle, windows smashed, yet in vibrant shades—deep violet, lemon yellow, cobalt blue, lime green—as if to defy their condition. Children were running everywhere, chasing our bus, the older ones with younger kids hoisted on their backs, none of them wearing pants, screaming and laughing as if we had interrupted a vast and private celebration.

Leaving the airport, we'd been warned: "Don't give them money. Don't pass out food. If you do, we'll be mobbed!"

We obeyed the instructions, but the moment we climbed off the bus at our hospital, swarms of kids, most of them no more than four or five years old, engulfed us, shouting in English:

"Give me one dollar! Give me one dollar!"

When we didn't give in, they lost none of their joyous abandon.

That was my first and lasting impression of Haiti—the joy, the laughter and squealing, the beaming smiles of bright white teeth. I remember it like it was yesterday. It was 2006, my first international mission as a doctor. Dr. Edward, one of my favorite surgeons, had agreed to let me and two other surgery residents join his Haitian American team on their annual mission to Haiti.

Every hospital has a distinct and unmistakable feel the moment you walk into it—welcoming, like a warm home, or institutional and unhappy. Hospital Sacre Coeur, our station in the town of Milot, was the warm and welcoming kind, though from the outside it appeared modest, even impoverished.

Our team stayed a couple of blocks away in dorm-style accommodations, where we doubled up and shared rooms. We spent the first day sorting out supplies and making a plan for the week. We scheduled more complex cases during the first half of the mission so we would be around during the patients' acute recovery phase. We also arranged to do longer cases in the mornings and wrap up the evenings with simple procedures.

The Haitian medical staff gave us updates from the previous year. They had prescreened patients to make our mission more efficient, already identifying who we would potentially be operating on. The next day there were already hundreds of people waiting for us at the clinic, with hernias and thyroid goiters, lumps and bumps.

From the start it was hectic. We worked long hours to get as much done as possible while also being mindful of not overworking our local Haitian colleagues. We'd be gone after a week or so, but this was their permanent assignment. Fortunately, we could perform most of the minor procedures without them.

As hectic as it was, it was far less mentally exhausting than medical school. On my first day in Haiti, as I finished seeing our final clinic patient, I said to myself: *This is what medicine should be. This is why I became a doctor in the first place.*

At that point I had my MD and was nearing the end of my surgery residency but wasn't yet fully trained. Even so, I had already seen a lot in the practice of medicine that didn't sit well with me. It's okay to make money as long as it's in line with providing quality care for everyone. And it's okay to follow rules and regulations, as long as they serve rather than harm the patient.

But too often during my training that wasn't my experience.

For the first time, in Haiti, I had none of those misgivings. I was practicing medicine as it should be. The most important person was the patient, and the patient's needs were our priority. I wasn't handicapped by an excess of guidelines and regulations created by health care corporations or insurance companies. A sick person showed up with a problem, we took care of it, and that was that. Medicine as a straightforward human service. The patient was all that mattered.

Beth, who was a year ahead of me in training, assisted Dr. Edward with the first major surgery. Before starting, she asked, "Where's the dictaphone?" Surgeons in the US use voice dictation to record their procedures.

One of the Haitian nurses set her straight: "Doc, we're at a rural hospital in Haiti—there is no dictation phone! We don't even have a *regular* phone!"

Back in the States we dictated an entire composition for each surgery, documenting every step—the sutures we used and each cut we made. In Haiti, no one cared for extraneous information. We simply jotted "right inguinal hernia repair without mesh" on a piece of paper and stapled it to the chart. Why would anyone need to know more than that?

Surgery in the US requires permission from insurance companies. If a procedure is delayed, the patient can suffer. And sometimes permission is refused. In Haiti, there were no such roadblocks.

There was also no VIP treatment. In the US I've seen patients like a politician's spouse or a local celebrity receive more antibiotics or get checked on more frequently than "regular" patients, simply because of their status. Some have multiple consulting specialists or personal doctors who stray from standard of care. This type of VIP treatment can have the paradoxical result of worsening a patient's situation. I saw none of it in Haiti.

Another stark difference was that Haitian patients had different expectations for the types of postoperative pain medications they would receive. We'd perform major procedures on them—exploratory laparotomies for bowel obstructions, excisions of large ovarian masses, chest tube insertions for deflated lungs—and all they expected afterward was over-the-counter pain medicine. Most American patients wouldn't tolerate these procedures without IV narcotics. My patients at home consistently receive more and stronger pain medications than patients who undergo equivalent surgeries in Samoa and Nigeria, South Sudan and Syria.

Pain is a universal experience. It's not that patients outside the US feel less pain, but their perceptions of it are different.

In some cultures, pain is a hardship to be overcome. In others, pain is a natural part of life, something that everyone experiences and that doesn't need to be feared and defeated. Understanding how different cultures perceive pain helps us better treat our patients.

Once during a mission in Myanmar, a patient presented to our clinic with a fungating cancer that took over 80 percent of his left hand. I overheard our nurse Tanny say, "Too bad we can't help this poor man."

"Why not?" I asked. "We can remove his hand, right?"

"Our surgeons don't do that procedure," she said, giving me a sidelong glance. "Or do they?"

I went to see the patient. After a brief assessment and some small talk, I offered him surgery as an alternative to wound care and antibiotics. "I can amputate your hand. Do you want me to do that?"

He immediately perked up.

"Yes," he said, grinning.

I consulted the oncologist on our team, who agreed. "If you're comfortable doing this type of procedure, I say go ahead."

I don't perform elective amputations at home, but on missions I'll do procedures that are not routinely done by general surgeons in the US. I would not attempt to do brain surgery in the States because there are neurosurgeons at my hospital. If I'm draining a head bleed on a mission, it's because I'm the only doctor around who has had the training. Same with managing patients with fractures—when there's no orthopedic surgeon on the team, I'll do what I can to stabilize fractures and salvage limbs. My patients might have a limp, but they'll be able to walk.

To do the amputation on the cancer patient I would need the proper equipment, but we hadn't packed a surgical saw. Arriving at the airport in Myanmar some of us had laughed at a poster of forbidden items; one was a carpentry saw with a thick red slash through it. Now I could use one.

I explained the situation to Cheryl, our local nurse and liaison. She eyed me suspiciously.

"What kind of saw do you need?"

"Ideally, an electric saw, but I don't expect we have that. I'd *like* to use a Gigli saw. But if you can't find a Gigli, then a plain carpentry saw would work fine."

Cheryl gave me a double take but a few hours later returned with one.

"I got you the saw. It's being sterilized right now."

Sure enough, it was a twenty-two-inch hand saw, something you'd pick up at Home Depot. It wasn't the sharpest, but it would do.

Since this was my first elective hand amputation, I planned it out in my head. I had to cut through skin, fat, and muscle, clean everything up, leave enough muscle and tissue to cover the stump, and then saw through two bones. I had to amputate far enough from the cancer so that he wouldn't need another amputation later, but also leave a long enough stump to fit a simple prosthetic. I knew the techniques for closing leg amputations and thought they should be transferable to the forearm. I was confident this could be done but wanted to think it through, so I drew out the amputation on paper to make the steps clear.

A good surgeon has to have the right combination of confidence and humility. She must have complete faith in her ability to do a procedure flawlessly and manage any complications. If she's going to operate on someone, she must believe she is the best surgeon available for the procedure or refer them to someone better. But she also needs to be humble because she's serving the patient and not her ego.

If you were to ask a room of surgeons who is the best among them, they would have no trouble naming number one. But they'd have to think for a while about who was number two and three.

I guided the scalpel across healthy forearm skin, tracing the simple "fish mouth" pattern that I had marked out. I found the arteries and tied them off before dividing them, so blood wouldn't spurt all over the place. Then I split tissues, fat, and muscles down to bone.

Surgery isn't as bloody as people imagine. That's not what's extraordinary about it. What's extraordinary is how intimate it is. We cut someone open, and our hands are in their guts.

If you swiped through the photos on my iPhone, you'd find multiple rainbows, a beautiful sunset, and a bright green lizard. And then you'd see a gallstone, a tumor, and a leg. My friends have photos of turtles, kids riding bikes, and sailing with friends. I have the double rainbow outside my window, followed by a thyroid, a ruptured appendix, a brain bleed, and then a plant my friend got me.

It's not a normal collection for most people, but for doctors it is.

On one trip to Haiti, we brought along a photographer named Faith to document the mission. She told me that she wouldn't be able to stomach taking pictures of anything gory. I invited her to watch my first surgery—I think it was a hydrocelectomy with hernia repair—and she was game.

"Okay, I'll see if I can take it."

She found the procedure fascinating, particularly the part where we removed a large hydrocele without causing it to rupture. Soon she was photographing surgeries all the time. I said to her, "Faith, don't forget you have stories outside the operating room to document too."

I didn't know how I was going to react to my first surgery in med school. I had seen two of my classmates faint while watching their first incision, so I was a little nervous. I made it through several surgeries before I finally passed out during a longer case. Not from queasiness, but because I was standing in the same spot for too long with my knees locked—a rookie's mistake.

I learned that good posture during surgery is crucial, because you're often standing in the same spot for six to eight hours or more. I also learned that the OR table needs to be at the correct height. On some missions the table height can't be adjusted, and I've had to operate while standing on a large suitcase.

How time passes during surgery and in the ICU fascinates me. A forty-five-minute appendectomy where I dissect out an obstinate appendix can feel intolerably long, while a four-hour surgery to remove a near-obstructing rectal cancer, biopsy the liver, and place a feeding gastrostomy tube can go by quickly. A twelve-hour day where four patients are admitted, three are transferred out of the ICU, and two pass away can fly by in a blink. Another twelve-hour day of managing twenty critically ill ventilated patients with sepsis or heart failure passes by in slowest motion.

Operating puts me in a flow state where I'm making moves without paying attention to my body. Sometimes I'll feel neck and shoulder aches at the end of a case. I'll do some stretches to loosen tensed-up muscles. This isn't always enough. If I've had an emotionally challenging day, the physical manifestations tend to persist.

Surgery residency was grueling, like being in boot camp for six years. Some of my classmates were weeded out; others realized it wasn't the life they wanted. To prepare us for the physical demands, every third day we pulled a thirty-six-hour shift. The last twelve hours were in the operating room. We learned to function with little or no sleep. We learned that amateurs practice until they get things right, but professionals train until we cannot get it wrong, because a surgeon's mistake can cost a human life.

Of course, we do make mistakes. But we train like mistakes aren't an option and, like most surgeons, I became obsessed with not making one. When I make a bad decision, I berate myself harshly. But I need to move on from it so my future performance isn't affected. If I can't stop thinking about the last patient, I won't be able to function.

Once I reached the radius and ulna, I scratched lines on the bones with a scalpel, dented them with the chisel, and sawed away. I had to use extra force, like cutting tough knotted branches. It took a couple of minutes. Then I filed the edges of the cut bones smooth and covered them with muscle and skin.

Tanny, the nurse who had introduced me to this patient, checked on him in the men's ward that evening, asking through a translator, "Do you want any pain medicine?"

"No."

Tanny asked, "Doesn't your arm hurt?"

He laughed. "Of course—Doc cut part of it off today!" His attitude wasn't *I'll tough it out*, but rather, *why would I want pain medicine?*

She gave him a couple of ibuprofens. "You can take two more before you go to sleep for the night." He seemed amused that we had offered them and didn't ask for the second dose.

To be on the safe side, we closely monitored his pain indicators. Both heart rate and blood pressure were normal. He didn't appear uncomfortable. He was calm and smiled often. He felt the pain, but his vital signs were normal.

Our pain sensors do not differ from person to person, but two people feeling similar pain can have widely diverse reactions. One patient has an elevated heart rate while the next patient does not. Even though our physical brains are similar, the way I see and experience reality is not the way you do. Even if we come from the same culture and have similar upbringings, we differ in all our perceptions and that includes pain.

On the Myanmar mission I operated on another patient to separate fingers fused together from an old burn. A few days later when we needed help loading equipment onto our bus, who showed up to lend a hand? The recent amputee and the man with the previously fused fingers, his hand bandaged, having been warned not to use it.

Tanny couldn't help whispering to me, "Isn't anyone with two good hands available?"

W e have more in common than we realize, but we are also much less alike than we often presume. When communicating with someone, I have to be sensitive to the fact that they will interpret what I say based on their personality and life experiences. This is especially true on international missions. When I sense that a patient or medical translator doesn't understand what I'm saying, I'll rephrase it, coming from a different angle.

Some families want a lot of autonomy in making medical decisions; others want less. Some patients and their families want me to tell them what to do. In that case I'll sometimes say, "If it was my father, I would …"

I had a patient around my father's age who presented with a large bowel obstruction from colon cancer. When I told his wife what I would do if he was my dad, she was relieved.

"Please treat him like your father," she said to me.

As we make our rounds in the ICU back home in Hawaii, I tell my medical students: "When it comes to medicine, we must take into account our patients' individuality and cultural differences. A fresh post-op patient in Myanmar may not expect pain medication, whereas in America this would be considered routine."

I introduced my students to Rafael, a patient in his early forties who had come to the ER because he suddenly lost sensation in his right leg. Rafael had an aortic dissection and was rushed to the operating room. The surgery went well, but we kept him intubated postoperatively while monitoring him closely in the ICU.

When we went to see Rafael, he couldn't speak because of the endotracheal tube. So he wrote on a clipboard we gave him, "What's wrong with me?" He remembered calling 911 and arriving at the hospital but nothing more.

Sasha, his nurse, gave him the news that he had had emergency surgery.

"And if you're wondering why you still have a breathing tube," she explained, "it's because there's a chance you'll need another surgery, and we don't want to keep taking it in and out."

Rafael was remarkably calm for someone who had a tube down his throat the size of a garden hose.

"His right radial a-line isn't working anymore," Sasha said to me. "It's clotted off or something."

I told her I'd place a new one on the left side.

"Hey, Rafael, I'm going to do a new IV in your wrist after we give you a little more sedation. That all right?"

He gestured at me, trying to write on his clipboard.

Sasha told him, "You can write to us after Dr. Wang is done with the procedure."

He scooted over to the edge of the bed and stuck out his left arm for me.

"So you're going to sit there and lie still and let me do it?"

Rafael nodded.

That was pretty cool because more often than not we have to tie people down or sedate them before putting in an arterial line. It took me a few pokes to get the a-line in his left wrist, but the entire time he was giving me thumbs-up with his free hand.

Rafael was the first US patient in a long while who reminded me of those I cared for on missions.

As attitudes toward pain are starkly varied among cultures, so are attitudes toward death. On my international trips, death is a part of life and not something to be afraid of. I don't know why so many Americans don't know that.

In the US, we obtain legal consent from our patients, especially before performing surgery, because of the potential risks involved. On international missions we continue this approach to protect ourselves, even though patients in other cultures are not usually as concerned about death or legal liability.

I'll explain to them: "I'm going to take out your tumor, but there's a possibility you might lose a lot of blood or even die as a result."

They'll respond with something like: "I don't need to hear all this. You're the doctor; I'm here to let you do whatever you need to do."

Sometimes I'll tell a patient, "I think it's risky to operate on you."

"That's okay," one woman said to me. "If I die, I die, but I want to take a chance on getting better."

Sometimes, if the risk is too high, I'll choose not to operate.

One patient in Myanmar died from uncontrolled bleeding after surgery for thyroid cancer. Her family was heartbroken, but they were also grateful.

"Thank you for trying," they said to her surgeon. "She wanted you to try."

Tanny told me, "We were all in tears, and the surgeon was beside himself. But the family took it better than the team!"

Occasionally we see this attitude in the States, but it's rare. Usually what we encounter is extreme resistance to the reality of death.

Don't misunderstand—the families I've encountered on missions aren't less sad than American families who've lost loved ones. They love and miss their family members who've died just as much as we do, but they don't react to death in the same way. Other cultures seem to have a greater acceptance of what they see as a natural part of life, as something we will all someday face.

When patients pass away in US hospitals, it's not uncommon for there to be a huge emotional scene as family members catapult from the "denial" stage to the "anger" stage. Relatives are sometimes so overwrought that we have to call security to keep them from lashing out at the staff.

In our society, death is seen as something to avoid at all costs. No one wants to talk about it, think about it, or see it. We perceive death as a failure, something that could have been prevented. So we do everything possible to keep someone alive—often barely alive—even if it means prolonging their suffering for months or sometimes years. We have the technology to do this, and we have the insurance companies to pay for it. So we do it.

We have specialists who focus on a particular part of the body. They may be able to fix that part, but that's not necessarily the best thing for the patient. It's like we're trying to keep a machine going even when it's clear the machine is no longer working.

For example, an ER doctor might call a surgeon to see a patient with trouble swallowing from side effects of chemotherapy for metastatic lung cancer. The surgeon may offer to give the patient a feeding tube for nutrition, a treatment that might not help and could even hurt an outcome.

As unbelievable as it may sound to those who don't work in the medical field, surgeons will sometimes say, "The surgery went well, but the patient died." This is not meant sarcastically. The surgery may have been technically perfect, but it didn't save the patient. A "good surgery" is much more than excellent technical skills and deft hands. It's also about knowing when an operation could improve the patient's overall condition.

The basic steps of surgeries are not difficult to learn: cutting, suturing, tying. Next is knowing how much pressure to apply to the incisions, how much tension to allow when suturing tissues so they can properly heal without being squeezed so tightly that they lose blood supply. Surgeons need to know how to link together multiple small technical movements in the proper order, and when to adjust the order to fit the operation at hand. It can be very complex.

I remember a very intricate operation in Haiti on a baby boy who had necrotic bowel from late intussusception (a portion of the intestine had telescoped into itself, cutting off blood supply). The patient was tiny, and the operating room lights were unreliable. I needed to think quickly and work fast. I decided to do the surgery in two phases. In the initial surgery, we resected the necrotic portion of the intestine—instead of connecting the two ends together, we sutured the ends closed so stool wouldn't spill into the abdomen. Leaving the intestines "in discontinuity," we used plastic cut from a sterile IV bag as a temporary abdominal closure (and as a window to check the viability of the remaining intestines). With the dead bowel removed, our pediatric intensivists were then able to properly resuscitate the boy and get him stable enough for the second surgery. Two days later, we reconnected his intestines and closed his abdomen.

"Good surgery" starts with whether the patient should have surgery in the first place. If someone suffering from cancer or septic shock and multi-organ failure receives technically flawless surgery but dies anyway, maybe surgery was not the solution for this patient. A good surgeon knows how to operate; a better surgeon knows when to operate and when not to.

Outside the US, it's more acceptable to allow death when life has exhausted its natural course. This is not to say that everything is better in other cultures. If that were the case, our presence on international missions wouldn't be needed. There is much that I prefer about practicing medicine in the US. We have excellent facilities and very well-trained doctors and nurses. But so often we're distracted by regulations and irrelevancies that prevent us from practicing medicine in the best way possible.

On my first mission in Haiti, I got a taste of what it was like to practice medicine without these distractions. It was just me and the patients. There were no bureaucrats standing over my shoulder with checklists of metrics and regulations that might or might not apply to the person I was treating. I regained the enthusiasm that made me want to become a medical doctor.

A week or two after I returned home from the trip, the paradigm shift I felt began to fade. I returned to the struggles of working in the medical industry: fighting with insurance companies, dealing with excessive paperwork, and facing angry patients who demanded pain medication.

"You didn't give me enough—I need more!"

Although I didn't show or voice it, I was angry back at them. I fulfilled my professional responsibilities, giving everyone the best possible care. However, I couldn't help silently screaming at the more irritating patients. Someone wanted an IV for pain meds because they had a small lump removed in the clinic. *I did a major surgery two weeks ago on a patient in Haiti and he wanted nothing! Not even an ibuprofen!*

I love practicing medicine, and it doesn't matter who my patients are. I love them as my patients, though I might hate them as my neighbors. Such divided feelings are common among physicians. In truth, I would prefer to be a doctor only for the people I like, but I believe everyone deserves health care. The person who has ruined their health through neglect or bad choices deserves the same medical treatment as everyone else, even if those choices are indefensible. I can easily separate my personal feelings from my professional responsibilities.

Still, that first mission to Haiti created a deep divide within me that only grew wider as the weeks and months went by, until it eventually became a permanent rift beyond repair. It wasn't as severe as the break that would come later on, when I returned from natural disasters or war zones and felt disconnected and even alienated from life and loved ones back in the US. I didn't experience post-deployment trauma when I returned from Haiti as I would after future trips, but the mission created a rupture nonetheless. I knew in my heart that I was meant to do international work on a regular basis, but every trip cost me time away from the work that paid the bills. How could I manage to do what I now loved most? I had to find a way to make it happen.

Chapter Two
Unwilling to Speak

I was born in Taiwan and grew up there with my parents and younger brother Rocky. We lived in a two-bedroom apartment on either the third or fifth floor. (There was no fourth floor in our building because Chinese people consider the number to be bad luck.) My brother and I shared one room, and my parents occupied the other. I remember playing with Rocky and our cousins, making up adventure stories as we crawled around behind our couch.

When my grandparents were young, they moved their families from mainland China to Taiwan to give their children greater opportunities and freedom. My parents met in college and got married after they graduated. My father worked at a printing shop and my mother stayed home to take care of us.

My dad used to tell us, "I learned everything from my father," even though his father, an artist, died when my dad was only eleven or twelve. I don't know much about my mother's early life. If I did, maybe I would have a better understanding of some of her ways. I do know she had seven brothers and sisters, and there may have been more siblings who didn't survive into adulthood.

My parents were in their thirties when they decided to move to the US. I was eight at the time and didn't understand why they were making this decision. All I knew was that I loved my cousins and didn't want to leave them. I had no inkling that we lacked anything in Taiwan.

What I did know was that my mom saw how hard I worked in private Catholic school and thought it was too demanding. "I saw you, a tiny girl in the second grade, carrying a heavy backpack full of books and assignments, doing your homework all the time," she said to me. "That's not how I thought it should be. That's why I wanted us to come to the US."

Opportunity for my parents meant less schoolwork for their children, not exactly the stereotype of the achievement-driven Asian immigrant family.

Before we left Taiwan, my cousin Lisa gave Rocky and me a crash course in English.

"How are you?"

"My name is …"

"I'm from Taiwan …"

That was about it. Maybe some Americans would know where and what Taiwan was, or be curious to find out.

When we arrived in San Francisco, we lived in my aunt's basement. Then we moved to a single room in the home of my dad's college friend. Eventually we rented our own place.

At my new public school in California, I was amused to see such a diverse mix of students—white, black, Latino, and a few Asian kids. It wasn't until I reached junior high and high school that there were more Asians in my classes. One of the first things I noticed was the strange variety of hair colors. Back in Taiwan, everyone had black hair. But at my new school there were all sorts of different hair colors—blond, brown, red, and even purple!

From the start I wasn't saying much. One day my classmate Yoshiko, who was Japanese American, carried a box of board games over to me during recess.

"Wanna play one of these?"

I nodded.

"You can pick one."

I scanned the games in the box and said, "Bingo." I didn't care much for the game, but it was the only one I recognized.

Yoshiko burst out laughing, and I was confused as to why.

"It's not pronounced 'bin-go'! It's 'biiing-go'!"

I stood there, unable to speak. I couldn't believe I was being made fun of because of my accent. I was so embarrassed that I didn't speak for the rest of the day. In fact, I stopped speaking English altogether for the next two years. I spoke Mandarin at home, but no English came out of my mouth until we moved to Maryland a few years later. Instead, I practiced in my head, vowing not to speak again until I was certain my accent had disappeared.

I doubled down and worked extra hard to read English at the level of my classmates. I was consumed with catching up to them, and I kept bringing home A's and O's for outstanding work. The teacher even gave me passing grades in communication although I didn't speak. The irony was that I was working as hard or harder than I had in Taiwan, which was what had disturbed my mom and prompted our move.

I was already a quiet and introspective child before the incident with the bingo game. I didn't speak much because I didn't have a lot to say. I believed that I wasn't as bright as my classmates. It wasn't until much later that I understood that being outwardly expressive isn't a measure of intelligence.

My dad tells this story about me. When I was around two or three years old, we moved to Tokyo because he got a job there. I knew some "baby Japanese" back then, but not much more. Dad was holding me on the balcony of our apartment, talking to one of his friends. That friend was also holding his son, who was about the same age as me, but much more animated. He kept babbling away while I didn't say a word.

"My son knows what airplanes are," said Dad's friend, beaming. "When an airplane flies overhead, he'll make an airplane noise."

"That's so cool," Dad said. Not long after, an airplane flew over us and the boy made airplane sounds. I burst out, "Look, an airplane!" I'm not sure whether I said it in Japanese or Chinese, but I knew the words. I was quiet, not because I didn't know the words, but because I preferred not to speak them.

Years later in medical school I learned about "selective mutism," a severe anxiety disorder where a child can't speak in certain settings while speaking fine in others. It described my experience exactly. For those two years in elementary school, I could speak only at home. I didn't think there was something wrong with me. Maybe if I had been given help, I would have been diagnosed with selective mutism. Maybe that would have gotten me talking sooner. But I'll never know for sure.

I'm glad that my teachers didn't try to get me professional help when I was younger. They let the problem resolve itself. Had I been diagnosed, labeled, and therapized, I might not have learned valuable lessons during my nonverbal years.

I wasn't miserable being mute. I simply wanted to sound like my American classmates and not be laughed at. My thought process was quite rational: "Okay, the problem is that I speak with an accent. I don't want to go through the rest of my life with one."

I thought it would be harder to lose my accent as an adult. I'd seen Chinese family members who'd moved to America when they were older struggle to lose their accents. I didn't want to go through that arduous process.

I was actually grateful to Yoshiko for pointing out my accent. I had no idea I had one. We ended up playing Bingo that day and became good friends.

My teachers left me alone, thinking I was slow to pick up English. I had no trouble communicating with the other kids. Talking is overrated. I pointed and gestured. I'd nod or shake my head or shrug. If the teacher asked me direct questions, I wrote my responses on a piece of paper.

If there had been a professional tutor available to get me up to speed in speaking, reading, and writing English, I would've jumped at the chance. If someone could have helped me speak accent-free English, I would have quickly signed up. But those kinds of services, if they were available, weren't offered to me.

I had a good friend in school named Judy Miller. She asked me straight up: "You can understand everything but just don't feel like talking, right?"

I nodded in agreement.

"That's cool," Judy said. No judgment from my good friend.

When I brought in my pet hamster for Show-and-Tell, I stuck a label on her cage: "Daisy, female Siberian hamster, eight months old."

"Does she let you pick her up?"

I put my hand in the cage and Daisy hopped on. The kids laughed.

Still, some of my classmates called me weird and tried to bother me. They would move my books around the classroom to see how I reacted. I just rolled my eyes and retrieved them. A boy named Caesar kicked my legs under the table when no one was looking.

I knew my vocal cords functioned just fine and that I was perfectly capable of speaking up if I wanted to. But I chose to remain silent and let them laugh.

As an adult, I'm quiet. I don't engage in conversations unless I have something to say.

When I was an intern, the chief of surgery told me that he liked me because I was a hard worker, but wasn't sure if I had the personality to do surgery because I was so shy. I was with Dr. Williams at the time, who broke out laughing. He was a general surgeon in his seventies, the kind of doctor who never retires. He said to the chief, "She's not shy at all! She just doesn't talk much."

I felt understood by that comment. I was quiet as a surgery intern because what was I going to say? Everyone knew more than me. I was there to learn. If I had a question, I had no problem asking it. I wasn't a silent nine-year-old anymore. I didn't talk simply for the sake of it.

Over the years I've learned that people are uncomfortable with silence, but as a kid I didn't know that people thought it was weird. I could spend hours reading a book or figuring out a math equation in my head. It may have looked like I was sitting there doing nothing, but that wasn't the case.

"Don't you have a book report due tomorrow?" Mom would say to me. "Shouldn't you get to work on it?"

"Yeah, I'm doing it."

"I don't see you doing it."

"But I am."

I was writing the report in my head before putting it on paper. That's what Dr. Williams understood about me. He knew that silence wasn't a problem, that there was a lot going on beneath the surface.

My brother Rocky, in contrast to me, liked to talk. He wasn't concerned about having an accent, and it went away very quickly.

While practicing English in my head, I spent a lot of time observing other kids and trying to read them. I learned how to tell a lot about a person from their body language. I could see in their eyes or in their walk that something was going on at home. I learned that nine-year-olds who share classrooms can have vastly disparate inner worlds.

Now, as a doctor, I use this skill to help my patients. Sometimes I struggle with verbal communication. I can't think of the right words or terms, and I have trouble describing or explaining things. But with my patients I have a felt, unspoken sense of how they're doing. I know when to pause and let them talk. And I can gauge how much information they want or need from me. For example, if someone has cancer, how much of their prognosis do I need to describe to them? Some people just need to hear me say, "You're really sick." Other people might want more information: "You have stage four metastatic cancer in your spine and there's a 95 percent chance the chemotherapy won't work."

Some doctors have no intuitive sense of their patients' feelings. My mom's gastroenterologist was one of them. He ate his lunch in front of us, talking about my mom's biopsy results with a fork in his hand. He said her prognosis was horrible and showed us graphic images of another patient's stomach cancer.

"Soon your stomach is going to look like this," he said, shoving a bite of sandwich in his mouth.

He had no clue that my mom didn't want to look at the images. All she wanted was for him to make the nausea go away. I was so angry I wanted to grab the fork and wave it in his face.

By not talking, I understood my classmates in a deeper way. I learned early on that "difference" bothers some people. We're threatened by things that we don't understand or that don't conform to what we think should be "the standard."

I didn't feel caught in some strange inner world or that I needed to talk more to make people comfortable. I wasn't thinking any of that. I felt like a normal kid, with a somewhat strange plan to sound like an American.

Two other incidents in elementary school had a profound impact on how I saw myself.

Not long after we moved to San Francisco I took a math test, probably in the fourth grade when I was eight or nine years old. That evening the teacher called my parents and told them I had cheated—I finished first, way ahead of everyone else, and answered every problem correctly.

"The only way your daughter could have done that was by stealing the answer key."

Looking back now, Mom probably knew I hadn't cheated, but she apologized to the teacher anyway (her English was limited, so it was easier to apologize than stand up for her daughter). When she got off the phone, clearly embarrassed, she said to me, "Don't do *that* again." She didn't say, "Don't cheat." Nor did she scold me. I was left to figure out what "that" meant.

What did I do wrong? What was so bad about getting the highest exam score? I must have done something that upset the teacher and my mom, but what was it?

Since I finished the test before everyone else, that must have been the problem. I thought I'd probably been showing off, so I decided to change how I took a test. I didn't intentionally choose the wrong answers; instead, I made myself a bit less focused. I learned to slow down so that I didn't finish first. I allowed myself to be a little sloppy so my scores wouldn't be perfect. Yet I still did well enough to continue to earn all A's.

A year later, my parents met with my fifth grade teacher. When they came home, Mom said to me, "Your teacher said you don't have to get straight A's all the time." She was giving me permission to be a kid because that was one of the reasons we had moved to the US.

As with the "cheating" incident, the message I got really affected me. Was something wrong with me for being such a good student? As before, I continued to put in less effort.

What they didn't understand was that I did enjoy life. Mom may have thought I was suffering because I spent hours every day alone in my room with a stack of books, but I had fun learning alone. I could spend all day and night doing one thing (drawing, painting, studying a subject I cared to learn, reading a book from cover to cover). Looking back now, I had an incredible amount of self-discipline and focus for a child—the makeup and personality of a surgeon and intensivist before I knew what they were. Maybe I also had the "wandering mind" of an artist.

Mom, a very social person, cared nothing for being alone and projected onto me her distaste for solitude. Maybe she thought I'd be happier if I played more and studied less. I could tell she thought there was something not right about me, which bothered me more and more in my teenage years and on into my twenties.

After those two incidents, I learned only what I wanted to learn from classes and ignored the rest. Despite that, I continued to do well throughout elementary school and junior high.

I continued to speak Mandarin with my family at home while watching sitcoms like *Three's Company* and silently imitating the actors.

I'd ask my cousin Lisa questions.

"Why does 'circus' sound like 'circles'? Is it because circus tents are round? And why does 'yield' sound like 'yelled'?"

She didn't have the answers.

As my dad drove us around, I instructed my little brother to holler "yellow" every time the traffic light turned that color, so I could understand how it was pronounced.

Rocky went wild every time we approached a stoplight. *"Yellow! Yellow!! Yellow!!!"*

Dad told him to shut up, but by the time we got home I understood the pronunciation.

Occasionally, as I felt I was slowly becoming accent-free, I translated for my mom at the DMV or asked someone in the grocery store, "Can you tell me which aisle has the toilet paper?" I'd talk to the librarian or order movie tickets. The people I spoke with had no idea that English was not my native tongue or that they were the first people outside my family I had spoken to in weeks. That gave me confidence.

By age eleven, I sounded (at least to myself, in my head) like a native speaker. I was ready to use my voice in school but wasn't sure how to begin talking in an environment where I had been mute for two years. Maybe I could start talking to my friend Judy and then everyone else.

Around this time my dad got a job in Maryland, and we moved across the country to a wealthy community so Rocky and I could attend quality public schools. We were relatively poor compared to a lot of the other families, but I never felt we lacked anything.

I left behind my mutism in California and started in my new school with no self-imposed constraints. I didn't talk much (there was no need), but I had no trouble speaking when necessary. Moving to a new school where no one knew me was a convenient way to break my silence.

People have asked me, "How did you know you didn't have an accent if you didn't hear yourself out loud?"

I learned to notice other people's slight to heavy accents, and in my mind practiced speaking without one. I could "hear" myself speak in my head. But I didn't know for sure how I sounded until I started talking two years later.

And when I did, on my own terms and timeline, I sounded "just like a real American."

Chapter Three
Aftershocks

When a catastrophic 7.0 earthquake struck Haiti in January 2010, I felt compelled to be there. The devastation I saw on TV was apocalyptic. The epicenter was just sixteen miles from Port-au-Prince, and at least two hundred fifty thousand residences and thirty thousand commercial buildings had either collapsed or were severely damaged. This included many hospitals. Port-au-Prince's morgues were overwhelmed with tens of thousands of bodies that had to be buried in mass graves.

Since my first trip to Milot with Dr. Edward's team four years earlier, I had completed my surgery training. I was now working as a trauma surgeon at a large hospital in the Midwest, where I was also the acting director of the trauma ICU. I arranged for some surgeons to cover my shifts at the hospital while I was gone, and in February went back to Haiti with a group of doctors and nurses from the Salvation Army.

When I got off the plane in what was left of Port-au-Prince, the stench hit me. Mounds of debris and rotting refuse were strewn everywhere. On the drive to our hotel we passed huge piles of rubble and buildings that were hardly standing. The presidential palace had collapsed.

We passed a long canal filled with sewage and garbage. I couldn't help but think about the outbreak of waterborne disease that would soon follow. With so many more mosquitoes than on the 2006 mission, malaria was now a real danger as well. People were sleeping in the streets, in their cars, and in makeshift shantytowns because their houses were either destroyed or in danger of collapsing. It was heartbreaking to think that this disaster could have been less catastrophic if only the country had stricter building codes. The shortage of fuel and potable water only exacerbated the situation.

Trucks rumbled through the streets, collecting thousands of bodies that needed to be buried. Thousands more were still trapped in the rubble, and the smell of decomposition was pervasive. Aboveground tombs were forced open so that bodies could be stacked inside. Others were burned. A Vodou priest called the lack of dignity in the mass burials "a desecration."

And yet the street children were still there—running around with no pants, smiling and laughing, although not quite as happy as the kids I saw in 2006. It was clear that they had experienced trauma. Almost everyone had lost a loved one. Many couldn't eat or sleep and refused to stay in their houses from fear. Whenever a small tremor shook our clinic, I saw petrified faces around me.

I had expected to be doing debridements—cleaning up infected or necrotic wounds by cutting off dead tissue. Or revision amputations, where I'd close open amputations to provide healthy stumps for prosthetics later on.

But we encountered none of those cases. We mostly did minor wound care, like I&Ds (incision and drainage) for abscesses or superficial wounds. I wondered whether the Salvation Army really needed a trauma surgeon on their team.

We saw many patients who, though they didn't have any visible physical injuries, wanted to see a doctor. Their psychological wounds were apparent in their body language. Their eyes were full of pain, and they all complained of headaches. With each aftershock they became more and more agitated, their eyes darting around frantically as they tried to figure out which way to turn.

I spoke with these survivors, reassured them, and gave them multivitamins because they were malnourished. Our interpreters thought I was a psychiatrist.

The Haitian people were extremely resilient in the face of the calamity, but probably all of them needed grief counseling and therapy. Very few, if any, received it. The psychological impact from the earthquake would be lasting, as it will also be from the COVID-19 pandemic.

We first stayed at a hotel and then at a school where windows were missing and some walls had collapsed. Aftershocks persisted for weeks, sometimes four or five in a row, big aftershocks. People on my Salvation Army team screamed, pulled out their Bibles, and called their families. The Haitians ran in and out of buildings, trying to guess where the danger was greatest.

I stayed put. The mosquitoes, which carried malaria, bothered me more than the tremors. The one time I was really scared was when a mob was banging on the outside gate of the school, trying to break in. They were enraged, and we were defenseless. I was afraid for the people caught up in the stampede and of what would happen to us if they broke down the gate. They didn't succeed and eventually went looking for shelter somewhere else.

There were ongoing gang wars in the city. One gang would offer international aid groups protection from a rival gang. There were stories of volunteers who were kidnapped and ransomed. I don't know if we had gang protection, but British troops and the US 82nd Airborne were supposedly keeping things under control. While we felt relatively safe, we made sure never to walk around alone.

The situation was made worse by the fact that many of the nongovernmental organizations (NGOs) that arrived didn't have a clear plan or avenue for how to help. At the peak of the relief efforts, the airport, with a single runway and only ten spaces for large planes, was in a state of chaos. Hundreds of planes transporting swarms of aid groups rushed to Haiti without designated landing times. Planes were landing or taking off every few minutes. There wasn't enough room on ramps to unload all the cargo. Some planes didn't have enough fuel to leave and found themselves stranded at the airport.

They hadn't communicated with contacts in Haiti to arrange for housing, food, or water, or to find out whether the help they could offer was actually needed. Our Salvation Army team tried to be as mindful as possible of our impact. We brought our own food and did our best to leave a small footprint. But I was aware that wasn't the case with many aid groups.

I was struck by the meager cooperation and communication among the relief organizations. With that much outside help, Haiti, a country the size of Maryland, should have been cleaned up in a month or two, but it took a lot longer than that. That was the hardest part to witness—the lack of organization and sharing of resources, so much waste and replication of effort. Some of the patients we treated had already been seen by another medical group the month before.

I wondered whether Haiti would have fared better without all the aid it received, and whether less outside help would have been more effective.

No doubt, there were many well-intentioned groups who genuinely wanted to help. But there were also NGOs who were more interested in marketing themselves: "We were on site in Haiti within hours after the earthquake …" This sort of negligent, not well-planned-out help is not uncommon on international missions. Groups show up in some countries to dig wells for natives who don't have them because they don't need them. Outsiders make cultural assumptions about what the locals need without considering whether those assumptions are accurate.

In the airport on the way to Haiti, I had heard chatter among my group.

"How many times have *you* been to Haiti?"

"Around six times."

"I've been there like *eight* times."

Was that a badge of honor? Compassion competition? Virtue signaling? This arrogance was and remains a dark underside to relief efforts.

At every Salvation Army station, a pastor was on hand to offer both medical help and prayer to patients. When a woman came in and declined the prayer, one of our pastors, Jimmy, was not okay with that. "Well, if a patient doesn't want prayer, they can't receive medical care."

I knew I had to challenge this rule, but Jimmy wasn't the kind of leader who responded well to women who pointed out problems or offered solutions he hadn't thought of. I'd had this experience before, time and again, in professional settings. If an idea came from a man, it had a chance of being implemented. But if a woman had the idea, we would have to worry about how to present it, especially if the receiver was male.

I've learned to be mindful of how I present concepts to certain colleagues and superiors. If they feel their authority is being challenged, they're more likely to shoot down the idea. So instead of presenting a proposal outright, I'll lead them to the idea by asking a series of questions. Or I'll let them believe the plan I'm proposing was inspired by them. I might say, "I got this idea from you last week when you said …" And sometimes I'll give a head honcho credit for a concept that was originally mine or from a team member to give it a better chance of being implemented.

I was on a COVID-19 deployment in Florida in 2020 with a disaster medicine team. The conditions we witnessed were horrific. My team members and I had ideas on how to improve the way we delivered care. As the chief medical officer, I arranged a meeting with the hospital's CEO.

The nurse supervisors had briefed us about the CEO and told us that talking to him would be a waste of time. We thought it was important to try. I brought two team members with me: Lena, the physician assistant who had been on the mission from the beginning, because she understood the deficiencies and could articulate our proposed solutions better than anyone. And Kyle, an ER doctor on our team, because he was tall, white, and male. We made sure Kyle wore his pressed battle dress uniform to the meeting.

The CEO looked at Kyle and said, "How can I help you?"

Lena spoke up first. "We've identified some process improvements for the COVID ICUs, and we wanted to talk to you about them."

The CEO continued to face Kyle, who looked over at me. I repeated what Lena had said, and Kyle nodded in agreement.

During the entire conversation, even though Lena and I did the majority of the speaking, the CEO kept his eyes on Kyle. If we hadn't brought him along, Lena and I might have been dismissed outright. Instead, the CEO listened to what we had to say, and we left with a commitment to discuss these process improvements in more detail.

When I was on a mission in Myanmar, Dr. Lum, our team leader, asked me to take care of a four-year-old boy with an infected cyst on his forehead the size of a golf ball. A monk in his thirties in a brilliant orange robe had brought the child in to see us. The boy was dressed in a similar orange robe and lived with the older monks; he, too, might someday become a monk.

"You can lance his bump with a bit of local anesthetic if you want," Dr. Lum told me. "Probably no need for sedation."

"Happy to see him after I get this sticky thyroid out," I said as I finished removing my third goiter of the day.

I was closing skin on the thyroidectomy patient when our nurse, Tanny, went to assess the little monk in the preop area. When I joined her and assessed the patient, I thought it would be best to give the boy a bit of sedation despite Dr. Lum's instructions, so I asked Tommy, a new anesthesiologist on our team, to help with the procedure.

He said to me, "I overheard Dr. Lum tell you to do this surgery without sedation."

"Tommy, this is my patient. I'd like him to have some sedation, please."

"Will you check with Dr. Lum?"

Although it was ridiculous, I agreed to do so. But I couldn't find Dr. Lum and wasn't going to chase around looking for him, so I asked Tommy to go ahead with the sedation.

"I'm sorry, I can't do that. Not unless you clear it with Dr. Lum."

I stood my ground as well. The boy and the monk who accompanied him sat patiently while Tommy and I went back and forth. In the surgery world, I can't force an anesthesiologist to give someone sedation. But Tommy's reason for not wanting to do sedation wasn't based on his medical judgment.

Lilian, another anesthesiologist, came by and asked us what was going on. She asked me how long the surgery would take. I told her that with sedation, it would be less than five minutes. Without, it would take longer and not be as pleasant for our patient. We would have to play with the boy and distract him so he would let me stab his head.

"I'll sedate this boy," Lilian said.

Tommy said, "No, I can do it."

Now the two of them were arguing.

The boy was eventually sedated, I forget by whom, and the surgery went smoothly.

I found out later that Tommy complained to Dr. Lum, who told him, "Cecily's the surgeon."

If I'd been a man, Tommy probably wouldn't have challenged me. That was one time I didn't hold back to spare a colleague's ego. I didn't change myself or try to be nicer. I stuck to what I thought was best for my patient. For the rest of the mission Tommy went out of his way to tell me how to do surgeries, including how to do an amputation.

Thankfully for me and the teams I work with, egos and personalities like Tommy's are rare on our missions. At the end of the trip, Dr. Lum walked up to me and said in a half whisper, "This will be Tommy's last mission with us."

Luckily, in Haiti, I didn't have to deploy any self-deprecating ruses with Frank, the lead pastor of our Salvation Army mission. He was very down-to-earth, and I could be myself around him without having to worry about filters.

"Frank, it's not right to deny medical care to patients who don't want to pray. We're here to help them, not turn them away. We can do prayer at the last station after they receive medical care, but only if they agree to it."

We adopted this process on the second day and there were no problems. Most patients still appreciated prayer. For the few who didn't want it, Jimmy could only roll his eyes and shake his head.

A man named Oliver came to see us. He was in his mid-thirties, tall and muscular, his arms covered in healed lacerations. He looked like a former soldier. There were no obvious clues about what was wrong with him.

He sat down and said through a translator, "I want to know how to stop hurting people."

I said, "Can you tell me some more about that?"

He spoke with a certain heaviness. "Before the earthquake, I was not a good person. I got into fights, beat people up, and raped women. I was put in jail, and these scars are from when the police tied me up and beat me. When I got out, I took some medicines and I was okay. Then the earthquake happened and I ran out of medicines. Can you give me medicines that will stop me from hurting people again?"

Had he been taking psych meds? I wasn't sure. He reached in his back pocket and, reflexively, I backed up a bit.

"Whoa, whoa …"

He held up a cell phone.

"See this? I stole it this morning."

I let out a breath I hadn't realized I'd been holding. What could I do for this man? We didn't have psych meds. If we did, it wasn't appropriate for me to prescribe them. Then I had an idea.

"Okay, come with me."

I took him by the arm and led him to the prayer station. The four of us—Oliver, me, our pastor Frank, and a translator—sat in a circle.

I said to him, "I want you to pray out loud. That way I'll hear whatever's going on in your head."

Oliver nodded and then began to pray. I listened to the translation.

There's a battle in my head. The devil is telling me to take that cell phone or beat up that person. I'm hearing these voices all the time. And then God or an angel is telling me not to do these things, but I don't know if I can listen. So I pray for you and I pray for me and I pray for the people I'm going to hurt unless I get help.

Frank then read aloud a Bible passage, talked about it briefly with our patient, and told him God loved him. Then Oliver looked at me.

"Okay, now what do I do?"

I gave him Benadryl, the anti-itch medicine that makes you sleepy. I dumped a handful of pills into a plastic bag and handed it over. The translator interpreted my instructions.

"You already have a layer of protection from prayer," I said. "This is an extra layer of protection from me. If you start to feel the urge to hurt someone, take one of these pills and wait twenty minutes. If the urge is still there, take another pill. You can keep taking them until the urge goes away. But first I need you to return that cell phone. This medicine won't work unless you want it to."

He nodded. "I'll try it."

It wasn't only the placebo effect I was relying upon. I was hoping the Benadryl would make him too drowsy to assault people. The risk of him overdosing was minimal. But I needed him to want the prayer-medicine combination to work.

Tara and I have been lifelong friends since seventh grade. We were both twelve when we met. I had just started speaking again after two years of being silent. We bonded over our shared love of philosophy and esoteric trivia. In one of our first conversations, I told Tara I didn't like the term "good, God-fearing folks." It seemed like an oxymoron to me.

She asked me, "What do you mean?"

"It sounds like people want to be good only because they're afraid of God," I said. "A person's goodness shouldn't come from fear."

I was raised Catholic, going to church on Sundays with my parents. They named me after Saint Cecilia, so you could say I was Catholic by proxy. I always hoped that someday I would understand what I heard in Mass. It's not that I was already an atheist; I was just a kid trying to figure out life.

I respected friends and family who were grounded in their faiths, even if I didn't always understand why they believed what they did. For example, should a person choose their "truth" based on whether they will be rewarded in the afterlife?

I find it odd when someone subscribes to a certain truth (whether it's religious truth or another kind) because that truth helps them. Not because it's the truth, but "because it helps me live my life." Why call it "truth" in that case? Why not say, "I'm using these principles/concepts/stories/teachings to guide me through life"? There must be something more to what we call truth. Otherwise, why not just follow whatever makes us happy?

Most religions are based on stories that may or may not be true. But whether or not they're true, followers accept them wholeheartedly. To believers, these stories are their objective truth and should be respected as such.

Tara is now the founder of an NGO serving people suffering from extreme poverty and malnutrition in Southeast Asia. She remarked to me one day, "You're a kinder person than a lot of Christians I know."

I took it as a compliment from my old friend, but it also struck me that I would never say to someone, "You're more tolerant than most atheists I know" or "You're more giving than a lot of Jewish people I know" or "You're the best Methodist I've ever met."

"You're Christian—you just don't know it," she said to me teasingly another time while we were flying to Myanmar for a medical mission.

"That's presumptuous on your part," I retorted.

I didn't think quickly enough to tell her that she was really a Hindu, just not aware of it yet, or that she was an agnostic but just didn't know it. I'm sure she would have appreciated the snarky tone. Friendly banter between us made the long flight to Asia go by quickly. I just felt badly for the woman who had to sit in the same row as us.

Tara looked over at me, no longer joking. "You have the same values as me. You believe in helping others, in being kind.

You told me you believe in showing up and bearing witness. Those are Christian values."

"Maybe they are," I said. "But maybe they're also human values."

Tara's love for Jesus is what drives her to do the work she does. It's why she founded her NGO and frequently goes on missions. Tara is a true believer, and her faith is what guides her actions.

I'm not Christian, but I don't think it matters all that much. I know that Tara would still be doing mission work if she had never heard of Christianity. Tara is a better human than I am, consistently kinder and more caring, while I can be "surgeon-y" at times, focused and aloof. But that's not because of our different beliefs.

When I was on a mission at the Syrian border during their civil war, I worked with Muslim doctors who assumed I was Christian. When they asked me about my faith, I told them, "I had the same discussion with my Christian friends in Haiti!" I could see the surprise in their eyes when they learned that I don't belong to any religion.

It's not surprising that religious people are often seen as good humanists. They have a set of morals and values to guide them. But do believers have a monopoly on helping people? Can someone be an agnostic or atheist and also a great humanist?

These issues come up for me because I'm a nonbeliever. During international missions I find myself among people with a wide range of religious views, in the local population as well as in the groups with which I serve. I am open to the possibility that I'm wrong, but I've not yet been convinced by any of the religions I've encountered. I've visited many different churches in my travels, and while I can appreciate the beauty of their rituals, I find that I agree with none of them. I am not convinced that any religion has found the truth.

I occasionally attend church back home with Christian friends, but the more exposure I have to various religions, the more of a nonbeliever I become. The younger me needed to know whether God exists. Now I'm more interested in discovering why some people believe and others don't than in finding out whether there is a God.

I do feel we have a certain obligation to not lie to ourselves and a responsibility to figure out the truth, no matter where that might take us. If we're content with living in ignorance, we're doing ourselves a disservice. It's not enough to just accept our differences; we owe it to ourselves and to each other to find out what is true. This is a personal journey that each of us must go on ourselves. We shouldn't expect others to go find the truth if they don't want to, though it's a little weird to me if someone doesn't have that desire.

I suspect all of us understand reality from within our own frameworks. Because people can have widely divergent, seemingly "opposing" frameworks, we experience divergent realities and we can never be absolutely certain about anything.

That's why I've always been skeptical of the Golden Rule of treating others as you would want to be treated. Why should I assume that others share my preferences? In many situations this is terrible advice that, if followed, can lead to unintended outcomes.

I imagine there are two kinds of "truth."

There's the truth that can be discovered, tested, and proven with science, logic, reason, and experimentation. As a doctor, I have faith in this kind of objective, scientific truth.

The world is round, flat, some other shape, or shapeless. Someone has cancer or doesn't. You're either pregnant or not—it can't be both. These truths can be tested, though the tests can be fallible. This is what I mean by "objective truth."

I've found that people tend to avoid the ugly truths that are right in front of their faces and choose to believe what they want to believe. I understand that it's human nature to want to avoid pain, and that sometimes we can be deluded about what's really going on. But I think it's important to try to see things as they really are, even if it's painful. Do we want to live our lives holding onto delusions or should we aim to shed them?

There is also personal truth or personal belief—the kind that differs for each of us based on our experiences. Some people believe in a literal interpretation of the Bible; others have faith in miracles. Some believe in multiple gods while others believe in one. A Christian, a Muslim, a Buddhist, and an atheist may all believe they've found "the truth"—but which of these truths is the correct one?

Objective truth and personal belief may not always align, but that doesn't mean either is invalid. Just because something cannot be proven scientifically doesn't make it any less true. We should be willing to accept new information and adjust our beliefs accordingly. There can be many ways for something to be true.

One day, when I was working near the station that provided Haitians with eyeglasses, in walked Oliver, the patient who had worried about harming others, wearing a clean shirt and new glasses, appearing so much more confident and less worried.

"Bonjour, Doctor," said Oliver. "I wanted to thank you. I returned the cell phone; I got these glasses to help me see, and I haven't had to use the medicines you gave me."

Frank, our mission leader, later said: "That was the most powerful faith healing I've seen in a long time."

I wasn't about to argue with him.

One night as we were sitting down for dinner at our hotel, Jimmy, one of our pastors, looked across the room and said, "Isn't that the table of Doctors Without Brains?"

This got a few chuckles at our table.

Encouraged by the response, Jimmy went on: "They're a bunch of heathens. All they care about is the medical part. They're in Haiti only because they want to be cowboys."

"Cowboys" is a term used by some to describe mission groups who act macho and recklessly, without an effective plan. These groups go to some of the most dangerous areas in the world, often at great risk to their personal safety. Doctors Without Borders (Médecins Sans Frontières or MSF, founded in 1971 by a group of French doctors) has a reputation for being one of these cowboy groups. They take big risks on the front lines, sometimes with dire consequences. Their facilities have been attacked and bombed, and their workers have been killed. In June 2021, three of their staff were killed in Tigray, Ethiopia. On various relief trips I've heard stories about MSF trucks being pulled over at gunpoint or their workers getting shot.

Relief workers with other mission groups are also killed but don't get as much publicity. My friend Amy's husband, during a mission in Haiti, went to the bank to deposit money for his NGO and was killed in a robbery. Their adopted Haitian son was left fatherless a second time (his parents died a few years earlier during the earthquake).

Jimmy didn't let up on mocking the brainless doctors. "And some of them are also homosexuals," he added, to knowing laughter.

The remarks didn't surprise me. I was aware of the rivalry and disdain between aid groups, as well as the homophobia in religious groups like the Salvation Army, and it deeply troubled me.

But isn't MSF also helping people? Why can't our two groups work together? Shouldn't we at least be sitting together sometimes?

Doctors Without Borders had a pediatrician, and we didn't. They had an infectious disease doctor, and we didn't. We had a surgeon, but they didn't. We could have referred patients to each other. Instead, we hardly acknowledged the other group existed.

I could only imagine the conversations at their table, until the night I overheard them talking about us.

"There's the Starvation Army table. They're more interested in evangelizing than in being doctors. I'm surprised they're not dressed like Santas and ringing bells."

Still, I made the effort to communicate with the MSF cowboys. I showed them a photo of an unusual lesion on a patient's leg and asked if it was caused by a fungus or a bug.

"Oh, that looks like a botfly rash," their infectious disease doctor told me.

I returned the favor. They consulted with me about a patient who had what sounded like a ganglion cyst on his hand.

"You can leave it alone if it's not affecting hand function or causing pain," I told them. "If it is, feel free to send him over to our tent station."

One of their doctors said to me, "You should be part of Doctors Without Borders. The faith-based NGOs want to convert people. We just want to do medicine."

I didn't think that was fair. The Salvation Army *was* providing earthquake relief. And Doctors Without Borders *wasn't* a group of unruly cowboys.

Yet some misconceptions weren't entirely unfounded. After all, one of our Salvation Army pastors did try to put prayer ahead of medical care. Doctors Without Borders did have a bit of swagger about going to the most dangerous places.

And yet we shared the daily mission of serving those in great need. By the end of the mission, we started to collaborate more.

As when MSF sent the ganglion cyst patient to me, who said, "I build things with my hands. I paint. But I can't do that because my hand isn't moving right."

I removed the cyst from his hand and a week later he returned with a gift—the first painting he had been able to complete in a long time.

As our month-long earthquake mission came to an end, I was left with a feeling of great worry for the Haitians. They were at extreme risk for waterborne diseases, as the canals were depositories for garbage and feces. The smell of sewage was oppressive. I feared that if something wasn't done soon, there would be a major outbreak of disease.

When I got back to the US, I wrote a letter in March 2010 to the American College of Surgeons:

I recently returned from working with the Salvation Army at a clinic in Petit-Goave, Haiti. While most of the acute earthquake-related surgical needs have already been addressed, I am concerned about the long-term psychologic impacts on the Haitian people.

I am also concerned about the emergence of waterborne diseases in the next few weeks. Attached is a photograph of a huge water drainage channel filled with trash, with hundreds of tents very close by. What will happen when the water overflows during a rainstorm?

Current efforts should focus on prevention of waterborne diseases. Future teams being deployed to Haiti should be warned of the new infectious diseases they will encounter; they also need to protect themselves.

The response I received was short and to the point.

"Thank you for your very perceptive letter. Is it okay if we publish it?"

I had been naïve to think that my letter might spur discussion and action in the medical community. By the summer, six months after the earthquake, as much as 98 percent of the wreckage remained uncleared. Most of the capital was still impassable, covered in rubble that held thousands of bodies. Some 1.6 million people were living in tents and tarps. Most had no electricity, running water, or sewage disposal. Crime in the relief camps was widespread, especially against women and girls.

Sure enough, around this time, Haiti experienced a preventable cholera outbreak. The media covered it as a second disaster, but it wasn't. It was a single disaster, an earthquake that didn't receive an adequate response. Why didn't we vaccinate all of Haiti against cholera? Why didn't we launch an effective clean-up effort within days of the quake? Instead, Haitians were told not to drink contaminated water. But what else could they drink?

It was such an impractical response, much like what happened during the COVID-19 pandemic. There was no real organized effort to prevent the spread. People were dying in droves and we could have squashed it, but we didn't.

Cholera is awful. Healthy people can suddenly find themselves dying from diarrhea and dehydration. They lie on cots with holes cut in them, and underneath there's a bucket to catch the rice water diarrhea that pours out of their bodies. They're being sucked dry by the disease.

Fortunately, cholera can be treated easily by hydrating patients with IV fluids and giving them antibiotics. So scores of groups now rushed to Haiti to provide these treatments. But by the time they arrived, there were already thousands of cases. People were already dehydrated and dying, and bodies were piling up again in mounds.

I experienced the cynicism that would return during future missions—some aid groups find it more satisfying to rush in and help after a calamity than to prevent one from happening in the first place. It feels more righteous (and perhaps more exciting) to fix something that's already broken than to quietly prevent damage. The point of international aid isn't for the "helpers" to feel good about themselves. It's to help.

I made a third trip to Haiti at this time with the organization of a famous actor. He had a house there and was helping to run cholera clean-up efforts. He also ran a well-organized tent city for houseless Haitians and was trying to network with other organizations.

I was treating cholera patients with fluids and antibiotics when I got a call that another group needed a trauma surgeon. A van came to pick me up. I climbed in after they unloaded IV fluids for our cholera patients.

"Hey, are you guys trading me for supplies?"

"Yeah, that's pretty much it exactly."

Now I was performing surgeries and managing ICU patients, the result of a collaboration that's too often missing in our work.

I met the famous actor a few times. The Haitians in his tent city hadn't seen his movies and didn't know he was famous. They loved him anyway and called him "the mayor" as he walked around, telling stories and bumming cigarettes. When they called him by his name, their pronunciation made me chuckle.

Cham-pain!

Cham-pain!

Cham-pain!

When I got back to the States, friends and coworkers asked me about him. *What is he like? Did you hang together? Tell us all about Champagne!* A few wanted to go on a Haiti mission to meet him.

It wasn't the first time someone told me they wanted to go on a mission "to have an experience." Friends have asked me if I could bring their teenage kids with me to give them a valuable life lesson. Some NGOs sell packages that blend volunteering with vacationing. Instead of going on a cruise to Jamaica, you can go to Kenya or Nepal to help on medical missions. Spend a week in Ecuador working at a clinic, and the last five days sightseeing and going to the beach. It seems disingenuous to promote these arrangements as helping those in need when, in reality, the vacation component takes precedence. What's more, it's often the case that the skill set of the volunteers doesn't match the needs of the communities they're purportedly there to help.

And there are nonmedical versions of these trips. You can go to Haiti and build a house from a kit that's shipped there. My friend Peter went on one of these "voluntourism" trips to Honduras with a Rotary Club from the US to paint a school. They partied the night before and were very late to arrive at the project the next day. By then local painters had shown up, which the school had planned to employ in the first place. Peter told me that instead of being embarrassed, the American team was offended. They made the local painters leave so they could paint the building.

Groups of Americans arrive to dig wells in a country where people walk for miles to get water. They assume the locals want wells, not bothering to find out why they haven't already dug them. Was it because they didn't understand the concept of wells? Or was it because they didn't mind the long walk to the river, which gave them a chance to conduct commerce and visit with relatives along the way?

If you want to make a difference, it may be more effective to donate to an established organization than to travel to an unfamiliar resource-limited place without a specific set of needed skills. Bearing witness to the difficult circumstances of others is important, but we need to be cautious about how we try to help.

Although Champagne was famous, I found him to be a down-to-earth mayor who had his finger on the pulse of the tent city. His group was also more organized and effective than some NGOs that had been around for decades, working with ten times his budget.

Chapter Four
The Harder Thing

My teenage years were tough. I argued a lot with my mother and she would hit me. Only after I left home did I have some insight into our unhealthy dynamic. I told my aunt Vivian that Mom and I had a major falling out, and that I was dropping out of college and moving back to Taiwan for a while. Hearing this, my aunt brought up the abuse, something I had never discussed with anyone.

"When your mom hit you and you didn't have a reaction, she became infuriated all the more and hit you harder," Aunt Vivian said. "Because you didn't cry or show any emotion, it made the problem worse."

I did have a reaction. It just wasn't visible. I thought if I showed any emotion, it would make my mom more upset. So I kept my face blank and my body still.

If Mom merely raised her voice, Rocky would show he was rattled. Like me, he didn't want our mother to be unhappy. He'd apologize or start tearing up so she wouldn't hit him. But I didn't apologize, cry, or show fear, which drove her mad.

I've always known my mother loved me, but I never really understood why she resorted to violence. The best way I can describe it is that she felt I was abnormal. She didn't approve of the way my mind worked. From a very young age I expressed perspectives and views that were contrary to what she thought a normal kid should have, and this caused enormous tension between us.

In my teenage years I started to realize that my relationship with her wasn't healthy for either of us, but when I was younger I didn't feel my mother treated me badly.

She indulged us, buying us things she couldn't afford and driving us everywhere we wanted to go. She signed us up for karate, piano, and tennis lessons. When we took up table tennis, she found us coaches from the Chinese national team. She traveled to tournaments and cheered us on at the Junior Olympics. She spoiled me and Rocky. My mother did more than her fair share of household work—cooking, washing dishes, laundry. Meals at our home were always delicious and healthy. My brother and I helped when we felt like it, which wasn't often.

One day my mother and I went into an eyewear store. The salesperson saw me looking at a pair of $100 Vuarnet sunglasses and said, "You people can't afford those."

I wondered which "people" he meant. Poor people? Chinese people? Poor Chinese people? Or something else? It bothered me more than if I had been alone because I was keenly aware that mom cared about our image. She was a proud and dignified woman who was now being judged on our appearance.

"Try them on," she said to me.

I put them on and looked in the mirror.

"Do you like them?" she asked.

"Yeah, they're nice," I said.

The sales guy was right—she couldn't afford them, but she bought them for me anyway, maybe to prove him wrong, or maybe because she wanted to give me everything. Although that wasn't the best thing for me, I did love those sunglasses.

In general, my mom was an amazing parent. She was easygoing when it came to rules, which made for a relaxed and enjoyable childhood most of the time. I didn't have a curfew, and while I wasn't praised for getting good grades, neither was I pressured to get them. I wasn't punished when I got an occasional bad score.

But I was a weird child that my mother couldn't figure out. If I did something she didn't like, said something she considered off base, thought outside her box, or was too precocious, too threatening—*whack!* Half the time I didn't understand what we were fighting about.

Our fights were rarely about rules being broken. Rather, they were sparked by our different perspectives and views. I was determined to make my own decisions, even when they went against what she suggested, an obstinate child who refused to be swayed. Yet I never fully understood why our disagreements would send her into a rage.

To this day, I can't remember the substance of a lot of our arguments. It's possible that the intensity of the emotions caused me to forget the specifics. I do remember thinking our differences were just that—differences—and not worth fighting over. I wasn't diagnosed with PTSD, but it's likely that I had some sort of adjustment disorder, considering what we went through.

In seventh grade the teacher asked each of us to pick our favorite animal. When she got to me, I said, "I don't know." I wasn't trying to be difficult. I simply couldn't choose, and the teacher became quite frustrated.

"C'mon, Cecily, you must have a favorite animal."

I said "elephant" to make her happy, so we could move on.

When I got home that night, I made the mistake of telling my mom about it.

"I don't see why I need to have a favorite animal."

"What? Every kid has a favorite. Cecily, I *know* you have a favorite animal. You're just not telling me!"

"I don't have one. I like too many animals."

I could have lied and made something up, like in class, but I couldn't bring myself to do it. Mom became more and more irritated, and from there things escalated.

I was stubborn and wouldn't quit defending my logic when we disagreed. The only way for my mom to end our debates was to hit me.

I didn't know why a parent would want to strike her child, but I thought if I shed tears my mom would feel remorseful and I didn't want her to feel that way. By not crying I thought I was being courageous and sparing her from guilt. But my stoic resolve just made her more infuriated. Instead of protecting her, I was unknowingly provoking her to hit me more.

Sometimes I would cry later on when I was alone.

I understand now that she was trying to regain a sense of control. She needed me to show some reaction, whether it was crying, flinching, or screaming. But when I didn't give her the appropriate reaction, I held all the power. I made her appear futile and impotent. Which made her angrier.

If Rocky disagreed with her, he would apologize and try to make amends. This was the response she needed. But I couldn't bring myself to be dishonest with her or myself. This was a skill that was not innate to me, that I had to learn in adulthood.

She didn't hit me until I was a teenager, around thirteen or fourteen. At first it wasn't too bad, just a slap across the face. But then it kept happening, a few times a week until I left home at eighteen. It was always over something stupid.

"Hey," she'd say, "why don't you have more fun?"

"I'm enjoying what I'm doing," I might reply, while reading the encyclopedia or nerding out with a trigonometry proof. But that answer didn't make sense to her. I had offended her by dismissing her suggestion to do something more fun than math homework. *Whack!*

"You're not supposed to be so serious," she'd explain. "You should be carefree and happy."

I didn't really understand what Mom meant by "carefree." It seemed like a lot more work to be constantly happy and flighty. And why did she want me to be less serious? I was happy with who I was, even if my mother couldn't see it.

We argued in circles until the only way to end the argument was for her to hit me. Then I went to my room or for a walk.

I had friends whose parents hit them, but the punishment they dealt out had logic to it. My friend Brie got the belt when she smoked, came home after midnight, hung out with a boy who was part of a gang, or when she lied about something, wore too much makeup, or forgot to do the dishes. I remember thinking, "If I was their daughter, I would know how to avoid being hit." It was clear why Brie was punished. I craved that clarity.

Many people who were abused will say that the physical part was the least of it. Being struck is fleeting, and the sting fades quickly. The greater trauma was from how arbitrary it was. I wasn't disciplined for behaviors. I was punished because I didn't think or act in the way my mom preferred, because our values differed. It would have been far easier to accept if I'd been punished for something I did and not for who I was—a child who didn't meet my mother's expectations.

I'd think to myself: *Why can't I have parents like Brie's, who make rules?* There would have been a logic to accept or reject. I could have chosen to be home before midnight to avoid a beating, or stayed out all night and accepted the consequences.

Instead, I was left to figure out how to avoid the next beating. I wondered if I should pretend to think the way Mom wanted me to.

Sometimes she used her hand on me. Other times it might be a hair-dryer or whatever object was within reach. She exploded from frustration. It wasn't premeditated; she felt pushed over the edge. I could sense that she felt badly afterward, even though she never once apologized.

She mostly hit me on the head, maybe because she thought that would stop my unconventional ideas. Sometimes she'd bang my head against the wall, not just once but multiple times. I have a hard skull, I guess, because I didn't end up in the emergency room.

(I did have severe headaches, although their timing did not correspond with getting hit. I believe they were physical manifestations of stress. I went to the ER a few times because of them, was treated with shots of pain meds, and sent home.)

I never fought back. When Mom was done, I'd go out for a walk or go to my room, where I'd cry or do something to occupy myself.

I ran away from home several times in junior high and high school, not for more than a day or so, not intending to permanently leave. I'd walk for miles to clear my head, through cookie-cutter suburban neighborhoods, along heavily traveled roads. My parents would drive around and find me, or someone would give me a lift home.

In seventh grade my friend Connie was away with her parents. She lent me her house key and I spent hours alone in her place, sitting and thinking.

No one seemed to take notice of what was happening, nor did I think to talk to anyone about it. My dad wasn't usually home when my mom and I fought; if he was, he went to another room and stayed there until it was over. Rocky, a superb table tennis player, had been shipped off to the Olympic training center in Colorado Springs when he was twelve or thirteen, one of the youngest athletes there. We didn't see him much for a few years.

My mother was not pleased when I told her as a teenager that I wanted to become a doctor. She thought my ambitions were childish and misguided, coming from where we did. In her world it was more prestigious to be an artist like my grandfather and father than to be a doctor.

"You're such a good artist," she said. "Why would you waste all that talent by going to medical school?"

She worked hard all her life so that Rocky and I wouldn't need to. She didn't understand why anyone would choose to work hard if they could have an easy life. She was worried that if I didn't choose wisely, I would end up being overworked and constantly stressed out. She didn't want me to make a foolish mistake that I would later regret.

She wanted me to have a comfortable life—become a well-respected artist, work at a non-stressful, non-demanding part-time job, find a husband to take care of me, live in a nice house, and raise adorable kids. This was what she had always wanted for herself, and it was her dream that I benefit from what had eluded her. Why would her daughter want to spend ten to fourteen years training for a career that demanded long, hard hours?

Because of her intolerance, I didn't experience a carefree childhood—the kind she ironically wanted for me. I was constantly on edge, not knowing which parts of my thinking she would disapprove of and lash out against. I was always waiting for her to find fault in something I said or expressed, and I braced myself for the explosions.

As much as I wanted my mother to be happy, she wanted me to be happy too. But she wanted a girly girl, and I wasn't interested in being a princess. She took me shopping to get me excited about new clothes. I tried them on, but I was just going through the motions.

"How about this coat? Isn't this a cute outfit?"

She wanted me to choose one and tell her how pretty it was, but I couldn't do it, even though my lack of interest was slowly ticking her off.

"Cecily, which of these dresses do you like better?" she asked, holding them up. I looked from one to the other, back to her, and then shrugged my shoulders.

"I don't know. I have a dress. I don't need more clothes."

"Cecily, you should be happy about this," she said, her voice rising in frustration. "Which one do you want?!"

I wanted neither. I had no idea I was being rude and unappreciative, but I hadn't learned how to navigate her feelings. And she hadn't learned how to deal with a kid like me.

Our family attended Chinese Catholic church almost every Sunday when I was younger. I enjoyed it because it was a time to socialize with my friend Brie, who I met at a church retreat. I also paid attention to the sermons, trying to understand why people believed in these seemingly irrational things. I hoped religion would someday click for me, but instead it became more nonsensical. I never rebelled or tuned it out; I just gently disengaged, like tiptoeing away from a sleeping dragon.

When I was fourteen I met Ryan, who was seventeen, at church. We hit it off and started dating. He came over to our house for dinner, and even though I soon realized he wasn't my type, for some reason Mom really liked him. She couldn't understand why I didn't like a boy who got along so well with our family.

"Cecily, you need to give him more of a chance."

"Not really, Mom. He's a nice guy, but I can't imagine spending an entire lifetime with him. I'd end up killing myself."

"Well, what's wrong with him?"

"I just know I don't want him for a life partner."

"Oh, Cecily, I can tell this is the one. You can have an amazing life with Ryan."

We fought over my unwavering desire to be a doctor, going around in circles, until, eventually, beside herself with frustration, she grabbed whatever object was within reach and took a swing at me.

When given the choice, I believe that a person should do the harder thing. When I was younger, I wrote in my journal, "Cecily, do the more difficult things!"

Even as a child, I experienced subtle but nagging negative feelings whenever I gave into the short-term pleasure of instant gratification. I experienced much more gratifying feelings when I practiced abstinence and waited for something better. I felt I was saying "Yes" to something more important, although I didn't yet know what that was.

Choosing the more difficult path has *almost* always been worth it to me. It means pushing yourself, taking on responsibility, growing in new ways, and living up to your fullest potential. When you make a habit of doing the harder things, life has a way of becoming easier.

When I was given the choice to go on a mission where I needed to speak French or one where I didn't need to know the language, I picked the French-speaking mission even though I couldn't speak the language. I tried to learn from a language app but was horrible at it, failed the French test, and didn't get to go on that mission. I felt pretty dumb, but I don't regret making that decision.

When I had the chance to return to work in Haiti or to join a team in South Sudan, I chose the latter because I felt I could have a greater impact there. I was familiar with Haiti, but South Sudan was more in need of a surgeon.

It became a discipline for me. There's gratification in abstaining from the easy choice. Instant gratification can bring more suffering than pleasure. If I do the hard thing, the next time I face a similar situation it's not that hard anymore.

But my mom didn't want me to take the more challenging path. To her, that choice was incomprehensible. If I went to college, why not major in an easier subject, like history or English? Why not become an artist like my dad and grandfather? Or get a low-stress job with a nice corner office and cruise my way through life?

So much more sensible than the life of a doctor. "Why would anyone want to pursue *that* life?"

When I was eighteen and about to start college, our fighting escalated to its worst point yet. One day my dad walked right into the middle of a furious argument. He saw my mom about to hit me again, put himself between us, and said, "If you need to hit someone, hit me!" For the first time ever, he stood up for me. I remember thinking, *Where have you been!?*

He never said anything to me about the incident, and that was the last time he intervened.

I spent a long time struggling with the legacy of my mother's abuse and my father's failure to protect me. I tried to make sense of why they would behave that way toward a child they loved. I had the impression that something was wrong with me, that I was flawed in some fundamental way, that the abuse was partially my fault. I'm nagged by the thought that if I had just given my mother what she needed, we both would have been spared the violence.

Why couldn't I say what she needed to hear? Why did I have to be so stubborn? I could have pretended to like Ryan, or raved about the dress she held up, or told her I wasn't sure about being a doctor. What was the big deal? My brother was a great kid and easy to raise. He knew how to appease our mother and avoid being hit. He gave her what she wanted, and I could have done the same.

I simply couldn't take that path.

Sometimes I'd try to reason with her: "Mom, I understand your point of view, and I'm okay with the way you think. I'm also okay with my own point of view. I would like for you to be okay with the way I think, with our differences." For whatever reason, that approach failed to work.

So I stood my ground, accepting her blows without emotion or complaint.

Something good came out of this. By doing the harder thing and not giving into her need for me to be a certain way, I became a much stronger person. When I meet people today who don't accept me, I don't lose confidence in who I am or what I believe.

The hardest thing to reconcile is that I still partly blame myself for not preventing the beatings, even though I was just a child and it wasn't my fault. I haven't been able to come to terms with these two divided parts of my psyche.

Chapter Five
Passages

I moved out when I graduated from high school and cut off all ties with my mother. I also stopped talking to Dad and Rocky because it would have been impossible to have a relationship with them if I didn't have one with her. I was now intentionally estranged from my family.

I majored in both art and biology at the University of Maryland, knowing I wanted to go to medical school at some point. I completed the premed requirements so I could have that option, but I was quickly disillusioned by how useless the classes were.

As a freshman in physics class, I was disappointed to sometimes score 130 percent or higher on exams. The professor added points to raise the class average, which made me feel that my hugely inflated test scores were meaningless. I stopped showing up to class and didn't take the final exam, and still ended up with an A because of my earlier test scores.

My performance was erratic. I barely scraped by in biochemistry. I failed the first exam and barely passed the second. I didn't want to repeat the class, so I studied to do well enough on the remaining tests to get through the class with a B.

Maybe my mom was right about medical school not being my thing.

After a major fight with my mother (about what I don't remember), I needed to figure out where I was going. So I dropped out of college and moved back to Taiwan.

I stayed in my aunt's place and taught English. I did some drawing and tai chi, and hung out with my cousins. Then my mom flew out and said, "You can't hide in Taiwan forever. It's time for you to come home."

I don't recall her being mad or confrontational. She just felt that I didn't belong in my aunt's house in Taiwan. And by then, I was in the state of mind to return. It wasn't my plan to move to Taiwan permanently. I knew at some point I was going to finish college.

Yet when I re-enrolled, I didn't have the motivation. I didn't feel like going to classes; when I did, I failed the tests. I dropped out a second time.

I was nineteen years old and unmoored, not knowing what I was going to do with my life. I took a series of unrelated jobs, from data entry and tutoring people in statistics to selling hand-painted greeting cards. I delivered newspapers, pizza, and subs. One of my friends owned a video editing company and I became a camera person, filming performances and weddings. After a number of months, I went back to college.

I adopted a stoic attitude toward my undergraduate classes: I didn't expect to learn anything important from them. I would learn by reading, talking to people, apprenticeships, and volunteering. My only goal was to get a BS degree so I could eventually go to medical school. And so I had enough drive to finish. I piled on classes the rest of the semesters and graduated four years after I initially enrolled.

I wasn't the most qualified candidate for medical school. My GPA wasn't a 4.0, and I did drop out of college twice. Rather than applying to medical school immediately after college, I started working, saving money and attending graduate school at night. As part of my strategy of "doing the harder thing," I worked as a copy editor for a scientific journal. I applied for the job, studied diligently to pass the grammar test, and took the position because it would force me to be a better reader and writer of English.

My mother had stomach cancer and a partial gastrectomy when we were still living in Taiwan. In her early fifties, the cancer recurred. When she was diagnosed the second time, I was working as a patent examiner for the US Patent and Trademark Office. I had seen my mom only a handful of times in the previous seven years.

When I went back home to help, I wasn't sure whether it was out of guilt or obligation or something else. I did miss my family. I went with Mom to medical appointments, found a fantastic oncologist, made a binder that organized her treatments, appointments, medications, etc. I also asked some of my good friends from childhood (who my mother knew) to visit her.

I didn't feel at home in my old home, but the environment wasn't unbearable either. It wasn't overly traumatic to be around her. She was now diminished, no longer the unforgiving and unapologetic adult who vented her wrath on me. I turned off the emotions when I was there.

At first I wasn't discussing Mom's poor prognosis with Rocky and my father, and I certainly wasn't discussing it with her. It was small talk or practical discussions about cancer management or plans for the next day. I avoided bringing up anything that might cause tension or an argument. Maybe Mom was doing the same.

She had metastatic gastric cancer with little chance of survival. She didn't want aggressive treatments or surgery if she couldn't return to functioning independently, but my dad wanted "everything" done. There were some conflicts.

I ended up becoming the de facto medical decision-maker in the family, even though I had a strained relationship with my mom. I hadn't applied to medical school yet, but I was already the "medical person" in the family. Dad and Rocky were softhearted and didn't know how to make the tough calls.

We finally signed up for home hospice after many long discussions about end-of-life care. The hospice service provided us with a lot of support.

I didn't have conflicted feelings about caring for my mother. But I did have conflicted emotions *while* caring for her. I'd play out various scenarios in my head. What could I have done differently? What could she have done differently? Could I have done more to help us get along without compromising my perspectives? How could we have communicated better? Was I wrong to leave my family? Had that been too drastic a step?

"You're not such a bad-looking person," she said to me one time while I was helping her get dressed.

Maybe that was her clumsy way of making amends for the past, for the times she wanted me to wear makeup or dress a certain way, when she kept reminding me, "Cecily, you need to look presentable when you leave the house."

On one of her last days, when she could barely move, my mother told my father that she saw light emanating from me. I'm not sure what that meant to her, but it made something inside me shift. Perhaps she was trying to let me know that she didn't hate me, that she had never really hated the way I was. Or maybe she was hallucinating from the fentanyl patches on her arms and back. Whatever it was, it meant something to me.

She died on her fifty-third birthday.

Among the confusing emotions was a sense of guilt. I knew of the connection between mind and body. I knew stress created stomach ulcers, which could turn into cancers. I knew our arguments were a major source of stress for her, as well as my long estrangement. She would have been less stressed if I had conformed to what she wanted, although I had no regrets for being the way I was.

Yet the feeling endured that I helped cause my mother's premature death.

I decided it was time to go to medical school. I didn't want to wait another year. Not being a traditional candidate, I applied to three Caribbean schools in July and started classes in August.

I was not as financially well-off as many of my medical school classmates and coresidents. I took out school loans, worked part time as a teaching assistant and tutor, and sold artwork to cover living expenses. Luckily, I didn't have to support my parents financially like many first-generation immigrants, which allowed me to save up a bit. Many medical schools forbid their students from working even part time.

When I started training, I was full of hope. I was going to be a doctor at last and provide quality health care to all! But soon enough, I started seeing things that made my conscience flinch. I was shielded from the worst of what I saw later on, but even as a student I could clearly say, "This is not how things should be. This is bad medicine, harmful to the patient."

What did I see?

When a rule doesn't make sense, there's a good chance that someone is financially benefiting from it staying that way. As Upton Sinclair once wrote, "It is difficult to get a man to understand something when his salary depends upon his not understand it."

Hospitals have what are called "quality metrics." In theory, this is a good thing. But in reality, some of the things doctors are required to do to meet metrics are counter to good medical practice.

In today's medical industry, we are often asked to prioritize meeting quality metrics over providing the best possible quality care to our patients. This can lead to suboptimal care and treatment, as well as ethical dilemmas that lead to decreased job satisfaction among medical professionals.

For example, one of the more important metrics is the number of "hospital-acquired infections." This number is a reflection of how good the hospital is at preventing patients from getting infections while under our care. This includes preventing catheter-associated urinary tract infections (CAUTIs), pneumonias, bacteremias (blood infections), and surgical wound infections. It is crucial for hospitals to do everything possible to reduce the number of hospital-acquired infections. What does not make sense is practicing bad medicine to avoid bad quality ratings.

A quality metric that is common and easy-to-measure is the number of CAUTIs. Hospitals take pride in the number of days/months with "zero CAUTIs." Doctors are encouraged to discontinue indwelling urinary catheters not because the patient no longer needs the catheter, but because they don't want to get "dinged" with a CAUTI. The longer a patient has an indwelling urinary catheter, the greater the chance of an infection.

We should remove catheters as soon as possible after they're no longer needed, rather than prematurely remove them to achieve a "zero CAUTI" quality score, which can result in skin rashes from urinary incontinence, urinary retention, and an inability to accurately measure urine output.

At some hospitals, the number of hospital-acquired infections is a metric that is kept low by limiting the number of sputum and wound cultures. To prevent or treat possible infections, doctors often give patients empiric broad-spectrum antibiotics. Sometimes this is done because it's the right thing to do, and other times it's done because doctors are pressured to refrain from ordering "unnecessary" cultures. The more cultures that are ordered, the more positive results will be found. Positive results mean infection, which can negatively impact the metrics. This creates a perverse incentive for doctors to avoid ordering cultures, and as a result, patients may not receive the best possible care.

Then there are patients who are "slow codes." This is when the medical team knows that a patient has no chance of recovery, but the family asks the doctors to "do everything possible." In these cases, the patient's code status is "full code" when it should be "allow natural death" (AND).

Some patients who have expressed their wishes for AND may have those wishes overridden. For example, once they are no longer able to speak for themselves, the surrogate decision maker or durable power of attorney for health might ask the doctors to "do full code."

I understand why the family would want to override a decision. They love their family member and want to do everything they can do to save them. But I have to ask the difficult question: "Isn't the decision your mother made back then what she would want now?"

I've overheard providers calling families to discuss the code status of their loved ones. It's a way to confirm the current code status. They're not trying to get the family to change their minds, but they'll say something like, "Do you want us to try and save your wife? Do you want us to resuscitate her, or honor the current code status?"

And then the emotions take over and the code status is reversed.

That's somewhat unnerving to witness.

I once heard an experienced charge nurse calling a family member.

"Your mother can't breathe. Her code status is AND/DNI (do not intubate). The ICU doctor is here. Do you want him to intubate your mother so she can breathe?"

After she got off the phone she said to the ICU doctor, "I don't know why they want you to intubate."

I thought to myself: *Maybe because you asked them? Why ask them to make the difficult decision under duress when they've already decided?*

When a patient's heart stops beating and their code status is "full code," the medical team has an obligation to resuscitate them. Even when it's futile, the doctors and nurses go through the motions. The patient gets chest compressions (CPR), epinephrine, and possibly a shock or two.

In real life, CPR is not nearly as successful as portrayed on television. In fact, most resuscitation efforts are unsuccessful. Yet, in the US, hospitals are expected to resuscitate patients who are full code. Sometimes when a person's condition is terminal, the code team will do a "fake" resuscitation attempt. On the rare occasion that the heart is jump-started briefly, it will stop again soon. This is bad medicine.

Although only a doctor-in-training, I was deeply disturbed by all of this but decided to focus on learning medicine. I saw medical school as something I had to do to become a physician. In the end, what really prepared me to be a doctor was residency. I learned more during my intern year than in all four years of medical school. Maybe later on, once I was in practice, I could do something about the many problems I saw.

This desire to reform the system has stuck with me. When COVID-19 hit, I hoped the pandemic would be an opportunity to uproot all the broken parts of our health care system and start afresh.

I wanted to finally see a health care system that was responsive to the needs of patients, efficient in its use of resources, and effective in its delivery of care. Sadly, the pandemic has not been a catalyst for the change I had hoped for. We still have a health care system that is too expensive, too bureaucratic, and too slow to adapt to the changing needs of patients.

I still believe that we can make the changes that are needed to create a health care system that works. But we need to recognize that the problems in our health care system are deep-rooted and that it will take more than a pandemic to fix them.

Chapter Six
Flies in the Coal Mine

The small plane descended. Below us was a treeless brown landing strip that looked rutted, not well-frequented. Moving specks on the strip grew larger, transforming into grazing goats and wild dogs; we were low enough to see their faces. The pilot buzzed the field a few times, raising dust. Once he scared the animals off the strip, we landed.

The first person to greet us was Zach (aka Bing), a retired general surgeon who was close to eighty at the time. He was a longtime member of Doctors Without Borders. It was 2014 and my first deployment with the group. This was also my first international mission not affiliated with a religious organization.

"Where in Africa have you been!?" Bing cried. "I've been waiting for you since last week!!"

There was only one flight a week to Agok; if the weather was rough, there was no flight at all.

Bing cut straight to the chase.

"There's this one guy we admitted a couple of hours ago, shot in the head." He pointed to the side of his skull. "Some of his brain spilled out. His vitals are fine, but he's probably going to die. Will you go check on him?"

Bing gave me a hug and climbed into the plane to head home.

After I dropped off my stuff at my new living quarters—I lived out of a single backpack for the next two months—I went to see my first patient.

His name was Yahya, and he was nineteen or twenty years old. His head was bandaged and he was in a coma, but he was breathing on his own and wasn't intubated. There was nothing I could do for him then; if he was still alive in the morning, we'd bring him to the operating theater and take a look.

After my first mission to Haiti, I found a way to work as a doctor and still have the time to do frequent international work. I did locum work, hired on a temporary basis by hospitals that needed trauma surgeons and ICU docs. The arrangement was perfect for me because it was steady, flexible, and paid the bills. I would pick up assignments for a few weeks or months, and then head out on missions.

After several more missions to Haiti, I applied to join Doctors Without Borders (Médecins Sans Frontières or MSF). I was attracted to them because they have no political agenda and don't take sides. They just provide medical aid wherever it's needed most.

Many Americans who work for MSF are retired physicians who need relatively little money. Others are young people who are willing to work for low wages. The pay is modest, especially compared with what we could make at home. For many of us it's not enough to cover our monthly expenses, like student loan payments or rent. I was able to save enough from locum jobs to work internationally for a large part of the year.

After I was hired, one of the first questions they asked me was whether I had a non-US passport, as it's not uncommon for MSF to run missions in countries where it's not safe to carry a US one. I told them I would renew my Taiwanese passport.

I was the only American on the mission in South Sudan and initially they worried about that. "You turned out okay," they told me later. "You weren't spoiled and judgmental, and you didn't insist on doing things your way." On our team were a Canadian, some Kenyans, a midwife from England, a couple of French guys, a Dane, a doctor from Mexico, and someone from Switzerland. We also worked with local Sudanese staff. In the middle of my time there, another American showed up.

It had taken about a week to fly to South Sudan from Hawaii. I went to Kenya first, spent a day there watching zebras and giraffes walk the streets, then flew on to Juba, South Sudan's capital, and from there to our compound at Agok.

The day after I arrived, Yahya was still alive. There were a few flies buzzing around us as I checked on him. Normally you'd expect zero flies in an operating theater. In Nigeria and Myanmar, Haiti and South Sudan, there are usually one or two. We're often in a room where the door can't close completely or a window is cracked.

We use the WSS (Wang's Sterility Score) to rate the air quality of our operating rooms. A room with five or more flies is considered contaminated and must be cleaned. Three to four flies are considered acceptable and we can continue working. One or two flies in the room is ideal. But if there are zero flies, we must proceed with caution because it's possible that the room cannot support life.

The flies are like canaries in a coal mine, so I didn't mind seeing one or two buzzing around me as I examined Yahya's entry wound—a tiny hole on the right side of his forehead. The exit wound, always larger, was in his left temple, large enough to expose protruding brain. I picked off some pieces of bone from the exit wound and cleaned it up as well as I could, trying to impact his brain as little as possible. Then I bandaged his head. We gave him antibiotics to decrease the risk of meningitis.

I emailed headquarters that Yahya might pull through, but for that to happen we needed something to cover the exposed brain. They didn't have anything to give me. I imagined their reaction to the email: "It's her first mission with us. She thinks she can save someone who was shot in the head? Not survivable!"

We weren't triaging Yahya—we weren't putting him aside to die. We only triage during mass casualty events. There was simply not much we could do for a head wound like his.

But Yahya was stable and breathing. I saw signs of improvement when I could look into the entrance wound on

his temple and see through his skull to the exit wound on the other side.

That might not make much sense, but a healthy brain is not close to the sides of the skull. Which is why, when you hit your head, the brain swings like a pendulum—when the front of the head is struck, the back of the brain can be injured. An injured brain swells to the point where it can come out the nose or ears or eyes. Because it was protruding from Yahya's exit wound, I made the hole bigger to release more pressure. When we could look through his skull, it meant the swelling had receded and the brain had returned to normal size.

The entrance wound, a tiny hole, had already healed within a few days, but the exit wound remained open. If we didn't cover it, he was at risk of developing an infection despite the antibiotics. I didn't want to use a bone graft if I didn't have to because that could also increase risk of infection.

So we improvised. I popped out the lens of my glasses and washed it, and one of the pediatricians donated his new shoelaces. We drilled holes in the lens and tied the shoelaces to it. Yahya wore the lens over the wound like an exoskeleton.

By week six, the exit wound was almost completely covered with granulation tissue, creating a big soft spot like on a newborn baby's head. I thought he might get through it after all.

We saw signs of improvement when Yahya started to have purposeful movements. First, his eyes began to follow our movements. Then he could follow simple commands, with his mother translating in Arabic.

Can you nod?

Can you squeeze my hand?

Yahya, now lift your right arm. Show me two fingers.

Move your feet.

He learned to sit up and then stand briefly, wobbling, with help.

Then he began to talk, responding to my broken Arabic with one-word answers. Wherever I go, I pick up a few essential phrases.

Do you have pain?

What's your name?

Are you hungry?

Where is the toilet?

He couldn't tell me where the toilet was, but gave appropriate answers to my other questions. Soon he was able to change his own dressing, although so slowly it was painful to watch.

To test his neurologic function in a different way, I played tic-tac-toe with him. I had the feeling he hadn't played before. I was told that he was educated somewhat and had been to school, but many other Sudanese weren't as fortunate. When I showed an eight-year-old Dinka girl a piece of paper and drew some shapes, she was fascinated. When I handed her the pen, she held it like a stick. It was clear she had not seen one before. Still, she managed a few tentative scratch marks on the paper. After

a couple of minutes, she was able to draw misshapen circles and squares. I let her keep the pen and pad. She would likely never have the opportunity to learn to read or write. While her mother recovered from burns, she was the sole caretaker of her eighteen-month-old brother.

To teach Yahya tic-tac-toe, I demonstrated with another person. Then I drew a new grid and marked a circle in one square. Yahya pointed to a blank square and I made his X. I drew another circle and he pointed to where I should put an X to block me. Soon he was playing well, blocking my moves consistently. He wouldn't put an X or an O in an arbitrary place. For the next few days we played a few games, and it got to where I could hand him the pen and he could make his own marks.

He slowly recovered. His exit wound healed and he could walk on his own. Time to send him home. I told him not to get shot in the head again. When it was translated, he gave me a polite half-smile. Not sure he got the joke.

It wasn't the worst injury I saw in South Sudan. The worst were the children who got shot.

Soldiers from an enemy tribe had raided a house when the parents weren't home and shot the kids. We worked on survivors who were shot in the arms or legs or butt. Children shot in the stomach didn't make it.

One toddler had several gunshot wounds to her buttocks and left leg. They weren't life-threatening, but her tibia had been shattered. The team was considering amputation.

She cried when her leg hurt, but generally she was happy and energetic, crawling around on her hands and knees. With six weeks left in the mission, we thought we might get her walking again and save her leg. We waited until she was well enough, then had her stand and put more weight on the leg day by day.

When I left the country, she was able to stand but not yet walk. I don't think the surgeon who replaced me amputated the leg, but I'm not 100 percent sure.

We treated a lot of burn patients in South Sudan, people who sustained extensive second- and third-degree burns from their cooking fires.

It's heart-wrenching to see severe burn wounds. As a doctor, it's the worst injury to witness and treat. Someone might have a C-section and go home the next day. But patients with severe burns can linger in agonizing treatment for months or even years, stuck in limbo between healing and dying.

The ideal treatment for severe burns is staged skin grafts, in which the patient's damaged skin is replaced with new skin. But we did minimal grafting because the patients were not recovering in the cleanest conditions. If the skin graft became infected, the patient then had a more grueling recovery along with more scars.

We were constantly improvising because we couldn't follow standard procedures. We were working on the ground without access to the same resources we had at home.

For example, I didn't do much for Yahya compared with what we might have done at home. I simply cleaned his wounds every day and gave him antibiotics. In the States he would have been operated on by a neurosurgeon, then spent months in physical therapy. Maybe he would have made the local news for surviving a gunshot to the head. What made Yahya's recovery miraculous was that he didn't receive any of these interventions and walked out of the hospital on his own, six weeks after arriving.

I'm not saying we should do less all the time. I'm not saying we should treat a gunshot victim in the US the way we treated Yahya.

But we often make the mistake of doing too much. The technology we have today can keep a rock alive in the ICU. Doing "less" to someone who is dying is often better for the patient and the family. Fewer surgeries and other invasive procedures, fewer painful needle sticks, and fewer tests can allow the patient more time to live.

This is a difficult concept to grasp because we are programmed to "do something" when we are faced with a sick patient. However, sometimes the best thing we can do is nothing.

I've become a better surgeon by working in hospitals in underdeveloped countries that don't have all the latest gadgets.

By learning to ask the right questions and using some simple but reliable tools, I've become more adept at my craft.

On missions I will hand sew patients' bowels together rather than staple them; operate with a limited choice of scalpels, scissors, and forceps; control bleeding with sutures rather than coagulation; and remove tumors by dissecting with my hands instead of with laparoscopic instruments.

More than once I've seen patients do better with fewer invasive procedures. And I've also seen people do well and recover with no treatment.

Yahya's case reminded me of patients in Haiti, when I worked with Project Medishare at a hospital in Port-au-Prince. The prostheses for amputees were kept on the second floor, and I saw recent amputees struggle up the stairs on one leg to get fitted. Then they'd run back down the stairs on their new legs, laughing.

I remember being stunned when I first saw that. How could they do that with zero rehab? Amputees in the States had to be laboriously taught how to walk again before they were allowed to attempt steps. But the Haitians knew none of that. Without a moment's hesitation, they plunged down the stairs, trusting their brand-new legs.

Chapter Seven
A Deeper Pit

In December 2013, less than two years after achieving independence, South Sudan rapidly imploded into civil war. The conflict erupted after President Salva Kiir accused his vice president, Riek Machar, of plotting a coup. This divided the country along ethnic lines, sparking bloodshed between Kiir's Dinkas and Machar's Nuers.

When I arrived seven months into the conflict, tens of thousands had been killed and over a million people—more than half of them children—had been displaced from their homes. Some five million people were in dire need of humanitarian assistance, according to UNICEF. The organization warned that tens of thousands of children could die from malnutrition. Within sight of our compound, there were about fifty thousand IDPs (internally displaced people) living in mud huts and cooking on open fires.

A dark aspect of the conflict was the violence against health care workers. Six clearly marked MSF facilities had been looted or destroyed in South Sudan in the previous eighteen months. The MSF hospital in Leer was almost razed, its maternity unit and storage area gutted by fire and its supplies stolen or smashed. Patients and medical staff were killed.

There were ongoing skirmishes, but we weren't in the middle of an all-out war. It was nothing like what I saw later during the Syrian Civil War. Our patients presented with gunshot and knife wounds, but we also treated a lot of routine medical needs like snakebites. About half a dozen patients had sigmoid volvulus, a condition in which the colon becomes twisted and requires surgery. There were midwives on our team, but I also did C-sections when necessary.

Most of our team members lived in cone-shaped huts (tukuls) that were more comfortable than those of the IDPs. Theirs were made of mud, while ours were made of cement. All the tukuls had thatched straw roofs, but ours were more durable. However, it would've been a poor allocation of money and resources to build cement tukuls for fifty thousand people.

There were no vacant tukuls when I arrived, so I was assigned to a shelter with metal walls and a tarp for a roof. Rain seeped through the tarp, and my mattress was continually damp. Every night there would be a ton of weird insects on my bed despite the mosquito screens. But on previous missions I'd dealt with extreme heat, slept in a tent, and gone without real bathrooms, so I told myself I could manage living in a metal container for two months.

We ate a lot of goat. It was tough and we tired of eating it all the time, to the point where peanut butter and bologna sandwiches tasted pretty good. On special occasions the kitchen staff might buy and slaughter a cow—an expensive indulgence.

I had four close friends: Anita, an English midwife; Elena, an ER doc from Mexico; Louis, a French logistician; and Buzz, a French technician in charge of water sanitation.

After a few weeks of living in my damp container, I wanted to go for a jog. Our compound was fenced, with armed guards posted at the front gates. When I asked if I could leave the area to go exercise, the guards told me, "No problem, doc."

But going for a jog wasn't that simple. A guard came with me, along with a few other people. They gave me a ginormous phone so we could always be in touch with the hospital.

The damp shelter made me achy and sick, and my clothes were always soggy. I wanted to tough it out but worried that my performance would be affected. Anita had an extra bed in her tukul, and I moved in with her for the rest of the two months.

Some days were very slow, with nothing much happening. There were rounds to make and patients to visit.

We were aware of the potential for violence between the warring tribes. We not only had guards with guns and a locked front gate, but also safe rooms. We felt secure, but the threat of violence always loomed in the background.

When we provided medical care to members of warring ethnic groups, we kept them separated to prevent potential tension. Occasionally a tribe member would show up at our compound looking for an enemy.

One patient had multiple infected abdominal wounds. His brother-in-law showed up toting an assault rifle and demanded angrily that we fix his relative and release him. He huffed and puffed, gesturing with his weapon. I had the sense he had been fighting since he was a child.

"We're doing everything we can," I told him, "but there's no surgery that can return him to normal. We're giving him antibiotics to fight the infection and doing our best to clean all the wounds."

It was scary for a few minutes until he backed down.

There were lots of kids running around, and we'd play with them during downtime. The girl who hadn't seen a pen before wore a tattered dress emblazoned with "Hello Kitty" on the front, so we called her Kitty. Her eighteen-month-old brother, tiny from malnutrition, we called Jack.

Their mother was in slow recovery from third-degree burns, healing and then getting infected again, so she couldn't care for them. Kitty became Jack's surrogate mom, carried him around constantly, and even tried to breastfeed him.

"You can't do that, sweetheart," we told her.

We taught Jack to walk, holding his hands. By the end of my time there he could take a few small steps.

The heat was stifling and the humidity was off the charts, like living in a sauna. But I got used to it, particularly after moving out of my leaky quarters. At night the frogs sounded an incessant chorus, and some people couldn't sleep because of how loud they were. I grew to enjoy the free soundtracks of white noise. You heard the frogs all the time, even in the middle of the day if you paid attention.

On my first day in South Sudan, a doctor told me a C-section story.

"There was a baby that was stuck inside the mom. They couldn't get it out in time and the baby died. I had to take out the baby in pieces."

There's not much I dread as a surgeon, but I dreaded ever having to face that situation. The thought of losing a baby is far more stressful than managing trauma patients.

And I've seen a lot of trauma. Gunshots, mass casualties, and holes in the head don't faze me anymore. I know that I'm doing everything in my power to help the patient. If a trauma patient doesn't survive, it's not because of anything I've done or not done. It's because the trauma got them. I'll be saddened, but I'll know that I did everything I could.

But losing a baby during a C-section is the stuff of nightmares.

I'm trained in doing C-sections but rarely do them back in the US. There are doctors who are better and faster at doing them than me. I wouldn't hesitate to do a C-section on international missions in an emergency situation, but the story of the doctor who had to remove the baby in pieces scared me.

On a mission in Haiti, I had to decide whether to perform a C-section on a pregnant woman who was dying. We attempted to resuscitate her but could not get back a pulse. She was carrying twins, and at twenty-two weeks their chance of survival outside the womb was almost zero. The majority of babies born at twenty-two weeks in the US do not survive, but at least they are given a chance by sending them to the NICU (neonatal intensive care unit). There was no NICU at our field hospital in Haiti.

Rob, the ER doc, said to me, "Do you want to do a C-section?"

It would have been a blood bath that everybody would have to witness, with almost no chance the twins would make it.

Rob saw my hesitation. "Shouldn't we give them a chance?"

"They have no chance," I said. "I'm not doing a C-section."

We covered the lifeless woman with a blanket. Her babies probably died a few moments later. Everyone was upset. I didn't question my decision at the time. A week or two later I wondered if I made the right choice. Had I been too hasty? Was there a way they could have survived? I still didn't think so, but the lump in my stomach lingered a while.

When I have a situation like that, I think I'm fine afterward, but I don't really know if I am. Maybe we doctors like to convince ourselves that we're fine even when we're not.

In South Sudan I went jogging one day and wasn't half a mile from the hospital when my phone rang. I was needed for a C-section. I ran back as fast as I could. I tried to prepare myself as I did with any surgery—I went through the steps in my head. I also asked the experienced Kenyan medical staff for help.

The mother was in pain, and the baby was stuck in her birth canal. I couldn't operate without family consent and in South Sudan that came from the husband. Everyone scrambled, looking for him.

If we operated without consent, we could get shut down. I was faced with an ethical dilemma, not my first by any means. As the director of surgery, the decision was mine to make.

I asked the project leader, "What would happen if I went ahead without consent?"

"That could be more dangerous to us, the mom, and the baby."

The obvious course was to operate, but it wasn't obvious in South Sudan. Both baby and mother might die, but all we could do was sit and wait.

We finally found the husband, got his consent, and wheeled the patient into the operating room. The anesthetist proceeded with the spinal block. We poured povidone iodine solution on her belly, and I pressed the blade of my scalpel through her skin and entered the abdomen. I then quickly cut into the uterus and carefully ruptured the fetal membrane, releasing a gush of amniotic fluid. A tiny pink foot was angrily kicking, to my great relief.

I reached my left hand around the baby and noted that his head was indeed stuck. I then used my right fist to push the baby's head back into the uterus from the outside. We cut the umbilical cord and I handed the baby to the midwife, who brought the wrapped bundle to the mother to meet her son for the first time.

There were lots of normal deliveries—far more than C-sections. After one I asked, "Do we give the placentas to the family?" I wasn't sure what the cultural practice was.

"Oh no, there's this big pit that we throw the placentas in."

I immediately became curious about seeing it.

One Saturday morning Anita and I were sleeping when we heard a knock on our door. At the window were Louis and Buzz, giggling.

"What do you guys want with us this early?"

"Wake up! We're going on a field trip."

We stopped at Elena's tukul and picked her up. The five of us set out on a rather long walk. We came to a concrete slab lying on the ground with lots of bugs flying around. Louis and Buzz lifted the slab and shone a flashlight into the pit. A mound of placentas. Then a second pit of sharps, followed by a third pit of body parts, looking like I expected them to look.

"Why did you guys bring us here?" I grumbled, my appetite for breakfast gone.

Elena also complained. "This was not a fun field trip."

"Well, you kept asking us to show you where the placentas end up," Louis said.

"I'll never be able to unsee this," Anita added.

Doctors Without Borders had been in South Sudan for two years. They thought they would dig these pits, be done with their work, and fill them up. That was our job—to make missions obsolete. But two years later the humanitarian disaster hadn't been solved.

"If we stay much longer," Buzz said, "looks like we're going to have to dig some deeper pits."

When there was downtime, we'd climb a long ladder to the top of a water tower. Being up so high was soothing, a way to relax and get away. Back in high school, even when I wasn't having a crisis with Mom, I'd escape to the roof of our house to have some time alone.

The water tower was our refuge, a chance to get away from everything and look at the view, which was lovely, even with the village of displaced people in the distance and the gray smoke rising from their fires. Whenever we had a rough day or someone died, we would climb the tower. Elena took care of more babies than I did, and almost every day there were babies dying. That's probably why we spent so much time on the tower.

Elena and I had our own language. A "workout" was our code word for doing chest compressions, a strenuous and often unsuccessful treatment. She'd say to me, "Cecily, I had a twenty-minute workout with an infant and it didn't go well."

When that happened, the babies were sent back to their families in shoeboxes we had brought along—cheap coffins on aid missions.

On the tower we'd talk about anything but our work, yet we couldn't get far away for long before another patient needed our help.

When my group was leaving South Sudan, those staying behind threw us a dinner party. Louis and Buzz, my close friends, weren't there. As we ate and talked, I wondered what happened to them. Did they smoke some pot and forget?

In the middle of the party, the two of them showed up.

"Close your eyes and put your hand out," Louis said.

I did as he said and felt a slimy wet thing in my palm. When I opened my eyes, I saw a tiny frog. I was so excited to see it, but it immediately jumped away.

They had been out searching for an hour because they knew how much I loved the frogs. Buzz was done, but Louis ran off to find another. He put it in my hand and once again it jumped away. Once again, Louis ran off.

When he returned, I was super careful. But still it jumped away—into a glass of bourbon. It swam around in the glass, slower and slower.

"I think he's drunk," Louis said.

We kept him for a little bit and then let him go.

"It made me happy to see you so happy," Louis told me, as we said our goodbyes at the gate.

Chapter Eight
Between Two Worlds

The culture shock I experience is not when I arrive in Nigeria or Haiti or Myanmar but when I return home.

In October 2014, after the mission in South Sudan, I moved to Hawaii. I lived the first year in an idyllic gated resort community. When the gatekeeper waved at me, I had flashbacks to the guards with rifles who protected our compound in South Sudan. The rows of townhouses were laid out in a pattern like our cement tukuls, but of course, the similarity ended there.

In my neighborhood we had more than we could ever need, while other parts of Hawaii had far less. I was back in a world of waste—wasted food, wasted energy, wasted time. I was living in a bubble, wrapped in layers of possessions, procedures, and technology.

In South Sudan I barely used my cell phone for two months and lived out of a backpack. Food, clothing, and shelter were basic and adequate. We didn't have toilets but used a hole in the ground. The women learned to pee standing up, using a funnel to aim our urine. No Netflix, Holey Grail Donuts, or Whole Foods. We ate goat meat every day. This week's pet was next week's meal.

When I return from a mission, I always make it a point to check in with my team members. I want to see how they're readjusting and if they need help. I often hear similar stories—that they can't bring themselves to spend $5 or $10 on a Starbucks drink because that's a month's salary in another part of the world.

I don't feel guilty for the luxuries I have at home. A bathroom and air conditioning are privileges that many people around the world can only dream of. What I do feel guilty about are the superfluous things, the multiple pairs of shoes and jackets. As a kid, I resisted my mom's efforts to get me new clothes when I already had enough to wear.

I tend to be an essentialist. Even though I do enjoy a few luxurious items, I own very few possessions. If I had to, I could fit everything I own into my car. Whenever I find myself with more stuff than I need, I downsize and give away my excess belongings.

I've met many people who remind me of what's important, even though their developing countries face severe problems. It's impossible to ignore the poverty, disease, and malnutrition that are commonplace in such places. But the people in these countries are so full of life. I realize that spending two months in South Sudan as a doctor is not the same as living there. The life I live is an extremely privileged one, and I am no more deserving of it than my patients on the other side of the world.

In Hawaii there's no shortage of luxury developments, upscale restaurants, and tourist entertainment. The wealthy folk here have more than they could ever need but still are not satisfied. They walk around like zombies in a fog. They're missing something essential that money can't buy.

When I'm driving in rural areas of Hawaii and see kids running around screaming and kicking a soccer ball, it reminds me of the kids playing in South Sudan as their parents recovered from burns and gunshot wounds. They were living instead of just existing or constantly longing for a better, imaginary life.

When I returned from South Sudan, I was back in the world of opioids, greedy insurance companies, and counterproductive hospital regulations. The health care system was a business, not a service to help people. The threat of poor satisfaction ratings from patients and lawsuits loomed over me.

I had trouble connecting with family and friends, and I also felt alienated from my patients. I was going through the motions with them, professional but detached. Like a soldier returning from combat, it was hard for me to readjust to "civilian life."

You're acting like you're the only patient in the hospital. You're demanding specific types and doses of pain medications, and now you're cross with your nurse because I couldn't guarantee a 100 percent pain-free procedure. I've been taking care of people in other parts of the world who have it far worse than you, and you have no idea how entitled you are.

I'd catch myself, reminded that the person I was taking care of grew up in the US, not South Sudan. It wasn't his fault that the US makes up 4 percent of the world's population and consumes over 80 percent of the world's opioids. It wasn't fair of me to think badly of a patient who needed better pain control. He was only expressing what he knew and what his body knew.

Yet I still missed being back in a world where nothing was taken for granted, where people were grateful for the smallest things.

I've been thinking a lot about medical relief work as I prepare for my next mission. Sometimes I wonder if I'm a "mission junkie"—someone addicted to the rush of helping others in difficult circumstances. Or am I simply called to work where the need is greatest?

I'm not sure. For me, international mission work is a priority. I'm one of the few doctors who works full time at home and goes on as many missions as some retired physicians. Part of the reason is because I don't have children to care for. But it's also because the work is so important to me.

I often think about the people we meet on our missions. They have so little, and yet they're so grateful for the care they receive. The work we do is humbling, and I feel privileged to be part of it.

Nevertheless, international missions have an addictive quality. There's something magical about them. Maybe it's the dopamine rushes we get from being needed and appreciated. Or the sense of purpose and belonging that we feel. Or the basic honesty of the work itself. We might witness horrific scenes, but on our return we miss the sense of purpose and camaraderie that went with it. For some, returning to mission work is the only way to experience that feeling again.

Our missions are planned months ahead of time. Knowing that I'm going to Myanmar or Nigeria or Samoa in a few months gives me something to prepare for. It grounds me. It gives order to my life.

Still, missions are meaningful for me, not an addiction. They provide a vital service to people who would otherwise go without medical care. They also remind me of how things should be, pointing to a purer, more compassionate way of practicing medicine.

People in developing countries seem to be happier with what they have, even when they have very little. Maybe it's because they haven't been exposed to the same level of advertising and materialism. Or maybe it's because they place a higher value on family, friends, and community than on individual possessions. Whatever the reason, it's something I wish we could learn from them.

Back in Hawaii, when I saw eight-year-old girls texting on their iPhones, I remembered the girl in South Sudan who had never seen a pen. Every night there I brushed bugs off my bed before going to sleep, and yet, despite my simple quarters, I slept very well to the murmur of countless frogs in deep conversation.

When I visited Haiti for the first time, kids would come up to me, touch my arm, and shout "Jackie Chan!" They hadn't seen an Asian person before. I wasn't offended. They were simply curious, and there was a genuine innocence in their reactions.

When I return from missions to countries with largely black, brown, and Asian populations, I almost forget the racism back home. Yet I'm quickly reminded of it when I return, another part of my post-deployment adjustment. I especially notice it on the mainland. I don't encounter prejudice in Hawaii, with its large Asian and mixed population.

The racism can be subtle. Sometimes it's a certain look from a group of people passing by. Or the vibes I get from body language. Sometimes it isn't subtle at all, as when someone, thinking they're out of earshot, makes "kung fu" sounds.

Since COVID-19, anti-Asian racism has gotten a lot worse.

My aunt Ingrid told me that she refused to leave her house in San Francisco during the pandemic. She said her Asian friends were harassed and had objects thrown at them, and she didn't want to be subjected to the same treatment.

For as long as I can remember, people have asked me, "Where are you from?" It's not usually said in a hostile way. Sometimes I'm not sure what the other person is asking at first. Sometimes I think the person is just curious. But it's led to some peculiar conversations over the years.

When I was a teenager living in Maryland, I was kayaking with my friend Monica (who is Caucasian) when we were approached by a boat with two white men. One called out in our direction, "Where are you from?"

Whatever happened to greetings like, "Good morning"?

I said, "Oh, we're from Rockville," to which he replied, "No, where are *you* from?"

I explained that I was from Maryland.

"But what's your nationality?" he asked.

I told him I was American. He asked about my parents.

"They're American too," I said.

"But where are *they* from? What's *their* nationality?"

"They grew up in China," I said. "What's *your* ethnicity?"

"Scottish and some Cherokee," he said. "I love China. My wife is Mandarin. Which part of China are you from?"

"I'm not from China!" I called out as Monica and I paddled further away. "I'm from Rockville! Nice chatting with you!"

"Don't you get tired of people asking where you're from?" Monica asked.

"Nah," I sighed. "I used to get upset when I was little. But we're surrounded by too many friendly white colonizer types—I can't walk around being offended all the time."

Occasionally, I'll make a game of it to entertain myself. I'll make up stories about them to explain why they're the way they are. Like the mostly white guy in the other boat. I imagined that his grandfather had sex with a Cherokee woman. And that he married a Mandarin orange.

I've been subjected to racism since I first moved to the States. People would talk "Chinese" whenever I passed. It could be kids in my classes or people on the street. It's always been there.

When I was around fourteen or fifteen, my dad and I were walking on the boardwalk in Ocean City, Maryland, on one of our mini vacations. We passed a boy who was about my age and his father. The boy did a fake Asian accent, clearly directed toward us. There were no other Asians around. His dad laughed. My dad didn't say or do anything, but I knew he heard it. If I had been alone, I probably would have kept on walking. But I turned to my father and said, "Hold on, I'll be right back."

I walked right up to the kid and his father.

"Excuse me," I said. "Fuck you."

I went back to my dad, and we kept walking without saying anything.

I used to think that racism was only perpetrated by white people. I saw them demean and belittle people of color, and I couldn't understand why. I now know that people of color can be just as racist as white people. I grew up around a lot of racist Asian people. My cousin preferred to date white men because he thought they were better than Asian men. My aunt would only hire Asian people to work in her store because she thought they were more hardworking than other races.

I think one of the ways we can start to manage racism is by acknowledging it. A big part of the problem is people who don't realize they're racist. We walk around saying, "I'm not racist. I don't see color; I treat everyone equally." But I don't think that's true for anyone, myself included. We all have implicit biases, and we need to constantly reevaluate our interactions and check the lens through which we see the world.

It's disheartening to come home from medical missions and go back to spending hours on chartwork instead of patient care. I love being a doctor in the US, but I'm spending less time with patients than I would like. Chartwork can consume several hours of my day and it's a difficult adjustment.

Another hard part of coming home is returning to the way Americans understand death. It's our job, by oath, to do what's best for the patient medically. We also promise families and patients that we will do what they ask of us. But these two promises don't always go together easily.

Not long after returning from South Sudan, I was working night shift in the ICU when I went to see a patient who was dying. His wife and daughter had visited earlier and they were begging him to "fight." The day shift doctor was their primary contact person, so my role was to just put out fires until he or she came back in the morning.

I peered into the patient's room to see how he was holding up. He'd had open heart surgery and multiple cardiac stents placed, but the surgeon and cardiologist had done all they could.

The patient's face crumpled when he saw me. "What are you going to put me through now?"

I gave him the news gently but straight up. "We're not recommending more procedures," I said. "If your heart stops, we won't subject you to chest compressions or intubation because those things won't help."

He knew he was dying and wanted his status changed to AND (allow natural death). He said he would talk to his wife, who would be visiting him in the morning.

When I told him he was dying, I sensed he felt relieved. Someone had finally acknowledged what he already knew.

The next night when I came on shift, the patient's nurse found me.

"That patient you spoke with yesterday? His wife was furious today. She said somebody told her husband he's going to die in three days."

"She's probably talking about me, but I didn't mention the number of days. I don't tell anyone exactly how much time they have left."

His wife was fixated on the three days. I was pretty sure no doctor or nurse had told her husband that. When I went to the patient's room, the wife confronted me, shouting.

"Nobody should tell my husband he's going to die in three days!"

I understood her pain. Losing a loved one is hard enough without being told exactly when it's going to happen.

"You're right, auntie. I'm so sorry," I said. (In Hawaii we often call older patients auntie or uncle.) "But his heart is failing."

She erupted in rage. "Did you tell him he's dying? Are you the one?"

I didn't have enough time to properly console her. I had other ICU patients who were waiting to be seen.

"I want him to fight!" she cried. "I don't want him to give up! You guys aren't God; you don't know when he's going to die!"

"He *is* dying," I said calmly. "He asked me about his options, and I told him. I believe he already knew. He just needed someone to affirm that."

She stalked out of the room. From his bed, her husband simply said, "I'm very tired."

We Americans tend to see death as an enemy to fight at all costs. But what exactly are we fighting? The people in developing countries don't cherish their loved ones any less. They celebrate the person's death in the same way they celebrated their life.

When I walked out of the patient's room, a nurse who heard the commotion asked me if I was okay.

"I'm okay," I said. "I'm just tired."

And it was mostly true. Okay enough to do my job well enough for the rest of my shift.

Chapter Nine
No Crying in the Operating Room

When we heard the bombs, we knew the wounded would be arriving soon. We rushed to the trauma bay and prepared as best we could. We were swift but calm and systematic. Did we have enough staff? Was our equipment in order? How many units of blood did we have?

In the United States our blood supply will occasionally run low but not for long, and we'll find ways to get patients the transfusions they need. That wasn't the case during the Syrian Civil War. There was never enough blood, and on that day we were particularly low. We notified the nearest blood bank to send us more units as soon as possible.

Then we waited, not knowing what the day would bring. Sometimes it was just a few patients. Sometimes dozens arrived all at once—a mass casualty situation. We had two operating rooms, two surgeons, one anesthesiologist, and limited blood products. We couldn't operate on everyone who needed it. Some would be helped immediately, but others would have to wait. What decisions would we soon have to make? What sacrifices? What compromises? What mistakes?

The ambulance sirens blared in the distance, drawing closer, and my adrenaline kicked in. I've responded to boat crashes, multi-car accidents, and even airplane crashes. You might think we would be overwhelmed in these situations, but that's not the case. We just do what we've been trained to do. During mass casualty events we remain cool, calm, and collected.

No one coaches medical students on how to manage their emotions while in the operating room. Those who go on to become surgeons have a way of ignoring intense emotions during surgeries, either not feeling them or not reacting to them. Someone who cannot function this way usually opts out of trauma surgery.

In the OR we don't let emotions interfere with our work. But afterward, when we're no longer in crisis mode, the emotional fallout sets in. It would be impossible to not be affected. The work takes an inevitable toll.

Sirens shrieking, the ambulances pulled into the trauma bay. A dozen patients were wheeled in and several needed immediate surgeries.

One was a boy, maybe nine. He had been crudely bandaged in the field, damage control to keep him from bleeding to death. He mumbled a few words in Arabic.

"He's cold," the translator said, "very cold."

It was winter in Syria and there was intermittent snow, but that wasn't why he was cold. His bandages were saturated with blood.

"What's his name?"

"Abdullah."

We wheeled him into the operating theater. I placed blankets over him and checked his vitals. He was stable. The anesthetist put him under; I gowned and gloved up. I gently peeled away the scarlet bandages to reveal a large diagonal slice across his back, all the way to his right buttock. Two broken ribs stuck out from the wound, bent back at unnatural angles. A gash in his diaphragm exposed his reddish-violet liver.

Shrapnel.

I washed the wound with saline and cleaned the skin around it. Then I stuck my hand inside and felt around. The liver had a little cut on it, not a big deal, and, miraculously, there were no injuries to his intestines. With nothing to fix below the diaphragm, I closed the hole.

I turned my attention to the broken ribs. One was so damaged it couldn't be saved. *All right, this needs to go.*

I wanted to use thin wires to reattach the remaining rib, but not having enough of them I used big sutures instead. I made two holes in the rib, passed the sutures through the holes, and tied it back in place to his intact ribs. Then I closed the wound but not completely because that could cause infection.

Next patient. Another kid, in a bright red shirt, maybe four or five, half an ear blown away, one eye swollen shut, cuts striating his face. Shrapnel again, most likely. He was lucky, considering what it had done to Abdullah. I squatted down beside him and he punched me square in the face, sobbing in Arabic.

"I want to go home! Take me home, take me home! I want to go home!"

A good sign: his brain was working. Much better than a silent five-year-old. He had no major injuries and didn't need immediate attention.

The next day he let me talk to him and peek under his bandages.

I was stationed with Médecins Sans Frontières in a small town in Jordan, about a mile south of the Syrian border, where the Jordanian ministry of health let us share a hospital.

It was January 2016. The Syrian Civil War, which started in 2011, is still ongoing as I write this, and has killed at least three hundred thousand civilians and created over thirteen million IDPs and refugees. And it's been dangerous for medical personnel as well.

A month after I arrived, Syrian forces and their Russian allies bombed an MSF-supported hospital in Maarat Al Numan in Idlib. Four rockets hit the hospital in two separate attacks, killing twenty-five people and wounding eleven. It was the third time the hospital had been targeted since the start of the war. In the months to follow, more MSF hospitals would be attacked.

As usual, our team of about a dozen was multinational— an anesthesiologist from Egypt, a nurse from Canada, an orthopedic surgeon from Denmark about seven feet tall. We looked amusing together; I'm about five feet two.

We'd get up at four or five in the morning and have breakfast, sometimes alone and sometimes together. Then we'd pile into cars and head to the hospital for our scheduled surgeries with burned or wounded patients. Then there were the emergency patients—soldiers, women, children, seniors—who could show up at any time, day or night. Although we were supposed to remain politically neutral and not treat soldiers, we didn't ask questions. We treated patients who, the week before, had been trying to kill each other. But in the hospital ward they hung out together, joking and playing cards, recovering from their wounds. There was one man who had been planting tomatoes when bombs fell and blew off his legs. Every time I saw him in the ward, he was smiling and kidding with the other patients. As was the fellow who lost both legs and one arm. "I'm thankful to be here," he told me. "I can't wait to go home to see my family."

Some of the patients sat outside. Passing them, we gave each other a thumbs-up or an okay sign. I knew enough Arabic to ask, "How are you doing?" One guy had lost an arm and had only three fingers on his remaining hand. His thumb was gone. So I gave him the okay sign with three fingers. That became our standard greeting.

We were treating war victims, so there was a clear need for medical treatment. I didn't have that sense of waste and replication, as on other missions.

A young man in his twenties, a grad student who I was told could speak English and Arabic, had an injury to his throat and chest. I gave him a tracheostomy and put him on a ventilator. One week later he woke up, barely breathing on his own.

We helped him learn to talk again. I gave him some balloons and hospital gloves to blow into so he could relearn to control his air flow. He could only text, not speak to, the love of his life, whom he had recently married. After a time he could kind of whisper. When he was able-bodied, he walked around helping other patients.

One day I found him in the men's ward.

"What's up? Why are you so happy today? What do you have to tell me?"

In a voice now stronger than a whisper: "I talked to my wife for the first time on the phone."

When Abdullah, the child whose back was sliced open by shrapnel, woke up from surgery, he simply said, "Thank you." Since the day he arrived, not once had I heard him cry.

Three months before I arrived at the Syrian border, in October 2015, the US bombed an MSF trauma hospital in Kunduz, Afghanistan, killing over forty patients and staff and injuring more than three dozen. Patients were burned in their beds; medical staff were decapitated or lost limbs. Others were shot from the air when they fled the burning building.

In the days after the attack, the US military claimed they had received reports that the hospital was holding active Taliban militia, before admitting the attack was "an accident."

Somewhere in the middle of our mission a new anesthesiologist arrived to join our group. Our project leader made the intros.

"This is Cecily. She's the surgeon from the US."

Instead of saying hi and greeting me warmly, as she had the others, the new arrival eyed me and simply said, "I just came from Kunduz."

She didn't hate me; she didn't hate all Americans. We got along fine, but she was letting me know that I should tread lightly around her.

Early one morning we were awakened by the sounds of bombs. We headed quickly to breakfast. Our project leader, Greta, who was Dutch, walked into the room. I was sitting next to Amr, the anesthesiologist from Egypt. People around us were eating and texting their loved ones at home.

Greta said, "Did you guys hear the bombs?"

We nodded and didn't say anything.

"You know what that means, right?"

We nodded again and ignored her. We all knew what the bombs meant.

Greta was irritated by our lack of attention and said sharply: "Am I speaking Chinese?"

Those at our breakfast table spoke several languages besides English—Greek, Spanish, Arabic, Dutch, Danish. I was the only one who understood Chinese.

I replied, "No, you're not."

The table broke into laughter. I hadn't intended to embarrass Greta. She glared at us and then said angrily, "Do you even know why we're here?" She stormed out and slammed the door.

The room became tense. This was the last thing we needed before a major casualty event. The next few hours would be crucial. The Danish orthopedic surgeon stood up and walked out into the hallway to pace, apparently his way of dealing with the stress.

We knew why we were there—not for "the experience" but to prevent people from dying. But I knew I needed to fix this before the wounded arrived.

Jenn, our lead nurse, was meditating in her room but had heard the door slam. I explained what happened and asked for her help.

Greta had to stay in the office to make phone calls, managing the team and ensuring our safety. It was a stressful job, but she wasn't in the trauma bay or checking on patients in the wards. A good project leader should help boost morale, not ask an obvious question and then slam the door on the way out. Jenn and I went to speak with her, to make peace for her sake and ours.

"I wanted to make sure you guys were ready," she said. "I felt you weren't taking this war seriously."

We explained that staying calm and having a sense of humor were our ways of preparing. We knew the storm was coming, so we hung out in the kitchen, chatting on the phone and eating breakfast calmly. There was no point in ramping things up before the ambulances arrived. We needed to stay calm and focused. We needed to laugh.

We made up and everything was fine. As Jenn and I walked away, we heard Greta mutter something in Dutch.

"What did she say?" Jenn asked me.

"Don't ask me," I said. "She didn't say it in Chinese."

The hypnotic call to prayer came several times a day, the first time at around four in the morning. Some people hated being awoken so early, but I welcomed it. Every dawn, that riveting cry was a reminder that I was still alive.

The house where we stayed had a roof we could access, and we made daily use of it to unwind, just as we scaled the water tower in South Sudan. It was the only place we could have honest conversations; in the hospital, it was work, work, work. If we had the time, we'd carry dinner up to the roof instead of shoving food in our mouths when we didn't have a moment to eat.

Amid all the death and destruction, sharing food felt like a family reunion and helped us stay human. The Jordanian nurses brought meals that their wives had cooked, or the doctors ordered street food from vendors—hummus, baba ghanoush, and marinated chicken. Sometimes they treated us with fries and hot dogs, their way of trying to remind us of home.

We could forget about the war and just be people eating together, enjoying each other's company, watching the sunset and sunrise, gazing at the stars. We'd chat about this and that, but right beneath the surface were our delayed reactions to what we had seen that day, the scenes we could no longer suppress.

When a mass casualty event occurs, there are no tears. It interferes with our effectiveness. We all learn to stuff down and postpone what we feel until later. It's amazing to me that, throughout my training as a doctor, our mental health wasn't ever discussed or addressed.

I tell my residents that it's okay to feel emotions and express them. I want them to be compassionate and caring people, not robots. If they need to, they can take a break and go somewhere to cry. I believe that's the healthier response.

But if you're operating nonstop on war-wounded patients, you can't give into emotions if you want to get through your day. You have to manage them. This leads to the usually unasked question: what's the best way for health care workers to do that?

During their training, therapists learn to deal with the intense emotions of their patients. They listen to patients talk about their traumas and use healthy methods to process the experience so they don't burn out from compassion fatigue. This is something physicians also need to learn.

Once I walk into the operating room, I'm not fazed by anything. I have a switch I can flip. The OR is a no-cry zone. I'm focused on the task at hand and intentionally suppress any emotions that try to well up. I don't have the right to cry while doing surgery because my job is to operate. Maybe dialing down feelings has become second nature. After all, I had a lot of training as a child.

I've seen frustration and anger in the operating room. I've also seen joy when a difficult procedure goes well. But never tears.

"We can't be sad in the OR," a transplant surgeon taught me when I was a second-year resident. "But we can be angry and still do surgery. Anger can give you the jolt of energy you need."

I remember him well; he was a good surgeon, but his style was to shout and throw things, a tantrum type of anger. I couldn't imagine how that would help me operate.

At the height of the COVID surge, we were very strict about allowing family members to visit the ICU. The only exceptions we made were for end-of-life patients. There was a man in our ICU who was nearing death, and his family members were coming in and out to visit him. But his son, around eleven or twelve, was too young to be admitted into the room. It was heart-wrenching to see the boy looking through the window at his father.

The ICU team allowed me to bend the rules and bring the boy in to see his father, even though our patient wasn't conscious. The boy was able to tell him that he loved him, hold his hand, and kiss him goodbye. It was a touching moment between a son and his father.

In the ICU, death is a constant presence. Patients die almost every day, and it can be difficult to find time to grieve in such an environment. Sometimes we have the opportunity to grieve with the patient's family, but other times we don't. I may have time to allow sadness to wash over me several hours after a patient has died, or I may not have time to process any grief.

Every now and then, when I'm not in the operating room or ICU, grief will sneak up on me. I'll get upset but won't show it. I've trained myself not to cry around others, certainly not around patients, even though they might see me on the verge of tears. If I'm going to cry, I'll go somewhere alone to do it— the bathroom or my car. Or I'll just wait until I get home. And sometimes I get so upset that I can't cry, like when my mom hit me so many years ago.

I don't go to the gym or take a long jog to decompress after a difficult shift. I used to drive around aimlessly for hours on end with no destination when I worked on the mainland US That's not an option in Hawaii, given its size, and it was certainly not an option on the Syrian border.

When I'm driving, I often find myself revisiting memories of past patients and surgeries. It's almost as if my body is reliving the trauma of that day. These forgotten memories come back to me with more clarity while I'm behind the wheel.

Now I walk more than drive. By the end of a walk my mind is clearer and more centered. I can release the memories and tension, especially if I leave my phone behind.

My brother is very good about not bringing his phone everywhere, which is the opposite of what I do. I'll bring it on a walk, and I'll end up answering emails or texts or doing work-related applications. This defeats the purpose of the walk entirely.

One day at our hospital on the Syrian border, the trauma bay was full of moaning, pleading war victims. A nurse held a wailing baby, while the infant's mother was bleeding to death from blast injuries to her right groin, the blood quickly soaking through wads of gauze packed in the wound. She had been injured shielding her child. The baby's screams overwhelmed the trauma bay.

"What do you want to do?" Jenn asked me. It was my decision to make.

The woman was pale and barely breathing, her pulse barely perceptible. If we attempted to keep her alive, she'd require a lot of resources—blood, mostly. The odds were very high she would die, while others might have a better chance.

The baby would not stop shrieking. I couldn't tune her out. I couldn't push it into the background. The screaming came at me from all sides, assaulting my senses.

"We'll take her," I said.

"We lost pulse," Jenn said.

We pounded on the woman's chest until her pulse returned. I extended her open wound to find the undamaged iliac artery, clamped it, and we rolled her into the operating theater. She died after using up all our blood supply.

That night we sat on the roof, looking toward Syria as the bombs fell in the distance. There was a war going on, but we found relief in talking about home.

"Hey, Cecily, what does your brother do?"

"He's a ping-pong coach. He trained at the US Olympic Training Center when he was a kid."

"Did he do ping-pong tournaments?"

"He competed at the national level and did really well. He stopped training after college and opened an art studio. Now he's coaching and painting."

We fell into silence, staring in the direction of Syria as night fell.

Jenn, sitting next to me, said, "Why did you take her?"

I didn't respond. I knew the woman had almost no chance of survival, but I resuscitated her anyway. Now our blood supply was exhausted.

"Why are we here?" Jenn said, more to the darkening horizon than to me. "Are we even helping?"

I wanted to tell her that we were, but I couldn't say it aloud.

When I got back to Hawaii from the Syrian border, I felt more profoundly affected than ever before. Our team members were encouraged to talk to mental health professionals about our experiences, but mostly we looked out for each other, calling and texting to check in.

But I was struggling with such a deep sense of estrangement and dissociation that I thought talking to someone might help. I checked in with our mental health worker. Unfortunately, I didn't find it to be very helpful. I decided to deal with my mental health on my own.

When people asked about my experiences, I had a hard time finding the words to describe what it was like. I wasn't angry at the questioner, but I didn't know how to explain the trauma to a friend or a family member. Or rather, the two traumas, which are quite distinct—the trauma of being there and the trauma of remembering.

Someone can have a traumatic experience that might not last very long—only a fraction of a second, or only a day. And yet the memory of it and its effects can last a lifetime.

In the trauma bay or operating room, we're focused on the task right in front of us. We know we can process the feelings later on. But that doesn't mean we're always able to do so once we're back home and there's time to remember.

Back home from the Syrian border, I was caught in the trauma of processing what I had suppressed. I had seen so many penetrating injuries, so many eviscerations, so many missing limbs. The limp bodies of dead children, the mangled limbs bent at unnatural angles. The uncontrollable wailing, sobbing children drenched in blood.

Bodily injuries, though severe, can often be managed with scalpels, sutures, and antibiotics. The most devastating wounds are the ones that can't be seen. The memories of working at the Syrian border, intense and disturbing, were more difficult to manage than being there.

I thought about my childhood and the hurt I felt when I was struck without knowing why. The violence was seemingly arbitrary. It felt like the world was a scary and unpredictable place. Now my career was based on trying to heal the wounds caused by arbitrary violence and natural disaster. Someone trying to psychologize me might say I'm trying to control and repair in the world what I couldn't control and repair in childhood. Perhaps there's some truth to that.

Eventually I allowed myself to grieve for the patients we lost on the Syria mission. One I vividly recalled was a young man with multiple shrapnel wounds. We cracked open his chest, opened the pericardium (the sac around the heart), and watched his heart valiantly attempt to pump blood that wasn't there. Even when the monitor showed us a flat line, we refused to pronounce him dead until his heart ceased to quiver.

It was hard to explain these experiences to family and friends. I felt numb and detached, going through the motions. I was disassociated and disengaged from others. Only those who had been with me at the Syrian border could understand.

The flashbacks continued. The twenty-two-year-old man who sustained blast injuries to his abdomen. He'd already undergone four laparotomies in Syria and had come to us with a gleam in his eyes, full of hope after having heard we could fix almost anything. When I entered his abdomen, I found that everything was matted together in a sea of guts and dense adhesions. Surgeons describe this as a "hostile abdomen." I couldn't tell what was small intestine and what was colon. He had two drains. I followed one to the segment of intestine it entered, carefully dissecting the scar tissue to avoid further injury. I followed the second drain to a large abscess pocket and drained it. Then I removed the clogged drain and placed a bigger drain in the abscess cavity.

We covered his intestines with a plastic sheet, laid blue towels and two suction tubings over the plastic sheet, then placed a second sheet of plastic over the blue towels to create a vacuum dressing. I decided to bring him back to the OR in a couple of days to take another look and give him an ileostomy (a place where stool can exit the body before the anus and be collected in a bag). This is done by making an incision in the abdomen, then bringing a section of the ileum (the last portion of the small intestine) up through the incision and suturing it in place to create a new opening, or ileostomy.

We operated on this man multiple times, even though he was succumbing to overwhelming sepsis and becoming weaker after each surgery. He asked us not to give up on him, and we asked him not to give up on us. We prayed for him every night. But after multiple operations, his body said enough. Even the ever-smiling Ibtisam, the Jordanian mental health specialist, cried.

And the man who came to us in respiratory distress from a gunshot wound to his neck. In surgery I found the bullet lodged deep. Miraculously, it had missed all the important major structures. He was one lucky dude.

And the fourteen-year-old boy with shrapnel injuries to his spine. We thought he was going to be paraplegic, but a few days later he showed our physiotherapist that he could bend his knees. I couldn't forget his grin.

After a few weeks back in Hawaii, I was sent photos of Abdullah, the boy whose back was ripped open by shrapnel. His hair was getting longer. I believe he needed one more surgery to clean out his chest. A few weeks later I received another photo of him back with his family, walking and largely recovered.

I thought often of the baby girl whose mother I failed to save. Of how I tried to offer her a balloon, only to watch her push it away and play with my iPhone instead.

During this time I did something strange. I bought a bulletproof vest and hung it in my closet. The chances of getting shot in Hawaii were virtually nil. I had seen a lot of violence during my surgery residency in Baltimore—gunshot wounds, stabbings, injuries from meth lab explosions, people who'd been set afire. Hawaii was tame compared with that. But after the Syrian mission, the vest felt like protection. Not from anything specific, but protection nonetheless.

Until the day I asked myself: *If I'm telling people I'm fine, why do I have a bulletproof vest hanging in my closet?* I dropped it off at a thrift shop, for someone who needed it much more than me.

Chapter Ten
Night Shift in the ICU

When I work the night shift in the ICU—6:00 p.m. to 6:00 a.m.—I arrive a few minutes early. The sounds at once envelop me—phones ringing, nurses taking calls, machines beeping.

"There's a patient in the ER who was just intubated," one nurse tells me.

"There's a patient on the telemetry floor who's crashing and needs to come down," says another.

"Dr. Wang, the patient in 314 is decompensating, but he's still refusing intubation."

Despite the surge in patients from COVID-19, I'm the sole intensivist on night shift. The nurses are also perpetually understaffed and overworked.

Our ICU has sixteen beds. Tonight, we have thirty patients. We've had to turn the third floor into a temporary ICU to fit them all.

My day shift colleagues look exhausted as they get ready to head home. "You okay?" they ask me. I tell them I am, although I'm not sure if I can handle thirty patients plus however many new admissions show up. If shit hits the fan, I'll call in the backup partner, even though he's already worked a full day shift.

John, a nurse, says to me, "Dr. Wang, we've been fluid bolusing this woman in 302 all day. Her blood pressure is still dropping, so we might need to start a second pressor. We'll need a central line."

John is doing his best to manage the situation, titrating her blood pressure meds every five minutes while also attending to two other critically ill patients.

And so my day begins—at 6:00 p.m. I stop by the west wing of the ICU to make sure that nobody is dying before I head to the third floor.

Janice is the nurse in charge of the west wing. Her face lights up when she sees me.

"Hey, Dr. Wang!"

"Hi, Janice. Is anybody actively dying?"

"No, we can handle it," she says, scribbling something on a folded piece of paper.

"There's a patient waiting in the ER who's too sick to be in overflow," I tell her. "Can we make a bed for her?"

Above her mask, I see a flash of fatigue in her eyes before it's quickly replaced by resolve. "We can downgrade a patient, but so you know, we don't have any open beds after that one."

As I'm going from room to room checking on the patients, Marcy, a travel nurse, pulls me aside. Since the entire state of

Hawaii is inundated with COVID-19 patients, we've recently received help from the government. FEMA funded five hundred travel nurses and some respiratory therapists to come work in our hospitals.

"I need to talk to you about my patient, Victor," she says.

Victor is a middle-aged man who suffered an out-of-hospital cardiac arrest two weeks ago. As a result, he has anoxic brain injury. His family has decided to withdraw support today.

"After everyone says their goodbyes, they'll be ready to extubate," Marcy tells me.

"Okay, thanks for letting me know." I change the order in the computer to comfort measures and write "extubate patient."

Having surveyed the main ICU floor, I head upstairs to check on the fourteen overflow patients. Nobody is actively dying. One patient needs another unit of blood, and another needs a different drip for sedation. It's a relatively quiet night so far, but there are many hours to go.

By 7:00 p.m. I finally make it to the patient who needs better IV access. She's a thirty-nine-year-old woman named Abbey who was admitted for sepsis from a nasty arm infection that started out as road rash from a fall.

"Hellooo," she giggles, grinning at me from behind a glazed stare. I suspect her giddiness is induced by the cocktail of pain meds we've been giving her, but regardless, I'm pleased to see a smile.

"Hi, I'm Dr. Wang," I say, smiling back. "I'm going to give you two new IVs, for these drips and to measure your blood pressure."

Her grin transforms into a scowl.

"They're not letting me eat," she says, not grasping the severity of her situation. "I've been here all day and those nurses aren't letting me eat!"

"You can't eat yet because you're very sick, and you might need to have surgery later tonight to clean up that arm wound," I tell her.

"The rude nurses are starving me!"

Her nurse, John, carries on, unfazed by the accusations. Unfortunately, our bedside nurses typically absorb the brunt of the patients' frustrations.

"How about this?" I ask her. "We'll give you some ice chips, and while you're snacking on them, I'll do the IV in your wrist."

That seems to placate her, and I start to set up the arterial line. But as she goes back into her animated, medically induced high, the procedure becomes more difficult. I've had worse—at least she's not screaming and trying to hit me. John and I try to distract her with conversation as she squirms and giggles.

The ER calls about another patient who needs to come to the overflow ICU. I put them on speaker as I try to quell Abbey's giggling fit.

"Dr. Wang," says a muffled voice. "We have an intubated COVID patient who needs a bed."

"Okay," I respond. "We'll make a bed for them in overflow."

After too many minutes of trying and failing to insert the a-line in Abbey's wrist, I give up and decide to place it in her femoral artery.

"You can have your ice chips, but please hold very still while I do this," I tell her. "The sooner we get it done, the sooner you can have your ice chips back."

Fortunately, she's not kicking too much, and I manage to place both the a-line and central line in her groin as John holds her leg still.

Time to check on the patient in 314, a young man—thirty-something, I forget his name—who's having trouble breathing and now needs to be intubated. He was signed out to me as "Severe ARDS from COVID-19 pneumonia, unvaccinated, on maximum high-flow nasal cannula." His nurse told me earlier that he had been refusing intubation, so we gave the high-flow nasal cannula a shot while I did Abbey's lines.

I give him the news gently but directly: "You're going to need the breathing tube to help you get through this."

"I don't want to be intubated."

I could say, "Okay, I respect your wishes. We won't intubate you. You know you will die as a result."

If he dies, it will open a room for another patient. I tell myself I can't be thinking that. It can't be part of my decision-making.

We keep going back and forth, and it's super frustrating. It's like arguing with a very stubborn cousin at a family dinner. I have to figure out a way to move on to the next patient because I don't have all night to debate him.

"If we intubate you …"

"I don't want it."

I persist because I believe he doesn't want to die. He's scared of intubation because he doesn't understand it. Maybe that's why he chose not to be vaccinated. I spend the next few minutes trying to understand him and build some rapport.

"My uncle was intubated and died," he tells me between breaths. I can see the terror in his eyes.

"I'm so sorry about your uncle," I tell him. "You have a higher chance of living with intubation. You will almost certainly die without a ventilator to help you breathe."

He glances at me with a pained expression and nods. He finally gets it. "I want the best chance of living."

It sounded so simple when I explained it to him, but it took forever to get to that point. I could have stopped at any point along the way and said, "Okay, I respect your decision," which would have been entirely understandable and professional. But if I had, he would have died a few hours later.

I have this sick feeling in my stomach that, by convincing him to be intubated, I might be denying care to someone who may "deserve" it more, like the woman who's been waiting in the ER for over twenty-four hours with a bowel obstruction. But then I take a step back and remind myself that I'm not denying the other person care. I'm caring for the patient in front of me— the only patient at this moment.

After I've completed my initial rounds looking in on patients and speaking with their families, I track down Dr. Smith, an ER doc who was looking for me.

"Hey, Lana, what do you have for me?"

She tells me about the woman in bed eight who underwent an outpatient endoscopy earlier in the day. The patient is seventy-four years old, has heart failure and chronic anemia. She received a unit of blood, then started having shortness of breath. She was complaining of not being able to breathe, so they sent her to the ER.

"We gave her Lasix, but she was still struggling," Lana explains. "I just intubated her. Can you take her?"

"No problem," I say. "But will you do me a favor and make sure she has decent IV access before transferring her up? I have like thirty-ish patients, and we don't have a nurse for her yet."

I walk back upstairs to look in on Victor. His family has decided to withdraw support, so I want to see if he's passed away yet. Marcy is there, tending to her other patients.

She says to me, "He's not extubated yet."

"How come? It's already been a couple hours since I placed the order. Victor needs to be extubated so we can open an ICU bed for Dr. King's patient."

"I thought the family wanted to be here for the extubation," Marcy says. "They made a big deal out of it, but they all left when I stepped out and now they're not picking up the phone."

Because of COVID restrictions, it wasn't easy to arrange for the patient's numerous family members to visit, but we let them come in small groups. Having them all return now would be a big ordeal. I start calling the family members one by one. Eventually, Victor's daughter answers.

"Hello, we haven't met. I'm Dr. Wang, your father's ICU doctor. I understand that the family wants us to remove your father's breathing tube. Would you like to come back and visit him before we do it?"

"I don't think I want to see him die," she says.

"I totally get that," I tell her. "I just wanted to check in with you first."

I tell Marcy to call me when Victor dies and head off to see Isabel, the patient in ER bed eight. When I show up, Manny, the ER nurse practitioner, greets me, his gown soaked with sweat. Dr. Smith had asked him to drop a central line before transferring Isabel upstairs to the ICU.

"I'm really sorry," he says. "I've been trying to do this central line for the last thirty minutes. It's just not happening."

Isabel's on a ventilator and sedated. But since Manny had trouble with inserting a central line in her neck, I decide to place both the a-line and central line in her groin, hoping to save time.

As I prepare to insert the lines, Dr. King calls again.

"Remember that patient I told you about?" he asks through the phone Manny holds to my ear. "Do you have room for him yet?"

"Sorry, not yet," I say. "I'll get back to you when we can move someone out of the ICU."

"No worries," he says. "I'll call you if he takes a turn for the worse."

After I insert the central line in Isabel's femoral vein, I spend what feels like an eternity trying to find her femoral artery for the a-line. I end up placing it in a tiny radial artery instead. I look through her old records and learn that she's had complications with her femoral vessels in past procedures. I should have taken the time to first review her records. I make a note for my colleagues so they don't make the same mistake.

The phone rings again.

"Hey Dr. Wang, sorry to interrupt, but we need to flip a patient. We're going to be gathering in fifteen minutes."

COVID patients on ventilators need to be turned every so often so all parts of their lungs receive oxygen. We call this "proning" and it can be backbreaking work, particularly when patients are heavy. To flip a patient who's hooked up to multiple drips and a breathing tube, we need several nurses, a respiratory therapist, and a doctor.

The patient we're about to prone weighs three hundred and eighty pounds. In some countries it's mostly men who are nurses because the job is so physically demanding. When I was stationed in Jordan, for example, most of the nurses were men.

Eight of us in gowns gather around the patient's bed. The nurses are lined up on each side and the respiratory therapist is at the patient's head, making sure the breathing tube doesn't become dislodged. I stand at the foot of the bed, ready to shout out the steps like a drill sergeant.

"Ready on your count," says Janice.

I begin calling out the commands: "Pull patient up toward the head of the bed ... now tuck his arms into position ... watch the Foley!"

The entire procedure takes about ten minutes and it's done with military precision. In the lull after the commotion, a heavy silence falls over the room. It's a sad sight to see the patient lying motionless on his stomach.

I head back to check on Victor again. Our respiratory therapist dashes out into the hallway.

"I'm really sorry," he says, rubbing his eyes. "I haven't extubated the patient yet. All right if I go give report real quick and do it right after that?"

He was supposed to end his shift at 11:00 p.m., but he stayed behind to help the nighttime respiratory therapist.

"Of course, that's fine," I say.

It's 12:20 a.m. I call Victor's daughter again. She picks up, sounding groggy.

"I wanted to let you know that we've removed the breathing tube. Your father looks comfortable. Would you like to come in to see him?"

"No, that's okay."

I place the order to move Victor out of the ICU while we wait for him to pass away. I call Dr. King to let him know that I finally have a bed for his patient.

"Don't worry about it," he says. "My patient is okay for now. He doesn't need to come to the ICU anymore. We can save that bed for one of your vented ER patients."

"Okay, but now I have someone for you. This patient came in two weeks ago. He was an out-of-hospital arrest with anoxic brain injury. We just extubated him and transitioned to comfort measures, but I don't know when he's going to go. I'd like to move him out of the ICU if you have a bed for him. If he goes while I'm still here, I'll take care of pronouncing and the death note so you don't have to worry about it."

"Of course," he says. "No problem."

Relief washes over me for a moment, but there's no time to rest. It's time to round on the patients again. I haven't seen most of them since I did my initial sweep.

At 4:22 a.m., I get a call.

"Hi, Dr. Wang. Victor just died."

I head upstairs to his bed. Lying there motionless, he appears little different than before. I pronounce him, and Marcy starts to clean him up and make him look good.

I call the patient's daughter. She doesn't answer. I call back two more times before she picks up. "Hi, this is Dr. Wang. I want to let you know that your father passed away peacefully. Would you like to come in now?"

"Yeah."

At last, a moment of quiet. I sit down as Victor is being cleaned. I brought a protein shake and a frozen dinner to work, hoping to eat it sometime tonight. I chug down the shake. Maybe I'll get to eat the frozen dinner tomorrow night. I should be going room to room to do one last sweep, but it's 4:45 in the morning and I need a moment to collect myself.

As I'm writing Victor's death note, Tony, a travel nurse, sits down beside me.

"Hey, doc, since you're here, can I ask you about my two patients?" he asks.

We make a few minor adjustments to their medications and tube feeds.

"How do you like being a travel nurse?" I ask.

Tony tells me that, although he loves being a nurse, he's planning to leave the profession after this year. He's been working as a travel nurse since last year and making $180 an hour, much more than the $25 an hour he made previously in Kentucky. With this income, Tony and his husband are saving up to start a shelter for homeless dogs. He says that many other nurses are in similar situations—they're not going back to their old jobs after this.

This is a common story. Travel agencies are contracted and funded by FEMA to find nurses to work for them. One agency not only pays its nurses $180 an hour, but when they work overtime—more than thirty-six hours a week—they can make $200 an hour or more.

With such high wages on offer, it's no wonder that many nurses are leaving their regular jobs to become travel nurses. Some have been going straight from nursing school to traveling because the pay is so much higher. Others are quitting their jobs altogether to sign up with an agency and return to their original hospitals as travel nurses. Why wouldn't they, when they can make four, five, sometimes eight, times as much money? This trend is happening with doctors too. Recruiters have been offering intensivists locum jobs that pay three times as much as their regular ICU jobs.

I understand why nurses and doctors want to earn more money. But the way things are currently going is not sustainable. Paying nurses to quit their jobs and travel has resulted in worsening nursing shortages. There's already a surgeon and intensivist shortage, particularly in rural areas and small towns. Sooner or later, something's got to give.

Hospitals across the US are struggling to keep up with demand as more and more patients flood in. This isn't simply a case of too few beds—we can always add more beds. The real issue is a lack of nurses, doctors, and respiratory therapists. If our state government responds by adding five hundred FEMA-funded nurses, our capacity is improved, but now the doctors and respiratory therapists are also overworked and burned out because of the influx of new patients.

One ICU nurse shouldn't have to care for more than two patients at a time. Even without the expected interruptions for studies and interventions, there's so much to keep track of—what patients are eating, their lab results, their mental state, what medications they need and when, their vital signs. One patient might be on aggressive chemotherapy, while another is dying with no family members present. In the middle of attending to one patient a family member might call, but the nurse can't drop what he's doing to take it. He'll have to call back when it's possible.

I don't know the answer to how many patients an ICU doctor can manage in a twelve-hour shift. Is it ten? Thirty? Fifty? But somewhere between ten and fifty is when we will no longer be able to provide quality care.

"People are accusing doctors and nurses of making money off COVID," Tony sighs. "That makes me upset. We were underpaid in the first place—of course we're not making money from COVID! But I can also see that something's off about what's going on with the COVID money."

I nod in agreement. "The whole thing is screwed up," I say.

I get a call that Victor's daughter has arrived, so I go to his room and find her sitting by his bedside holding his hand.

"He looks at peace," I say.

She nods. I talk to her for a little bit and then leave to make sure everybody is tucked in. The daytime doctors will arrive soon. It has been a relatively quiet night.

On the way home I stop at Holey Grail and reward myself with a $4 donut because, miraculously, only one person died.

I hope tonight will also be calm.

Chapter Eleven
First, Do No Harm

During the pandemic, health care workers became increasingly aware of the problem of "moral injury." We witnessed firsthand the devastation wrought on our patients and their families because of decisions based on greed rather than human welfare, and the result was an overwhelming sense of despair.

Moral injury is the term for the damage done to a person's morality or ethical framework from witnessing or participating in an event or situation that goes against their personal values. It's a state of being utterly exhausted and demoralized psychologically, a state more damaging than being physically overworked.

Many health care workers were already struggling with moral injury before the pandemic, but COVID brought all the system's flaws fully into the light. We saw how our patients suffered because of the callousness of those in power, and it took a toll on us.

I've never felt morally defeated on a medical mission overseas. I might be exhausted and emotionally depleted after a long day, but I don't feel like I'm complicit in medical wrongdoing. However, during the pandemic we health care workers found ourselves practicing in ways that went against our moral compasses. We became angry at the system that allowed this to happen, and also at ourselves for not being able to do more to protect our patients. We found it difficult to face ourselves, our spouses, and our loved ones. Some of us quit our jobs or got divorced. The aftereffects of this emotional disturbance will linger for a long time.

The Hippocratic Oath that physicians swear by—"first, do no harm"—refers not only to how we treat our patients but also to how we take care of ourselves. If we can't do both, there will be harm.

Navigating the pandemic has been soul crushing for so many of us. Millions died, and an unfathomable number have lost family, friends, jobs, and homes. There were so many restrictions, many of which made no sense. What we knew about COVID-19 was changing every day. We would adjust and correct our practices based on new information, which sometimes meant that we contradicted ourselves. And sometimes we were wrong because, well, science is not exact.

Many people blamed the medical system for their pain and losses. Health care workers were afraid to walk outside their hospitals in scrubs for fear of being attacked. We were doing our jobs and trying to minimize the effects of the pandemic, but to some we became the enemy.

Patients who were suffering from COVID-19 pneumonia were reluctant to receive treatment because they didn't trust it. I spent a lot of time trying to convince them to get the help they needed. I'd finish a long ICU shift, sometimes working thirteen or fourteen hours, and then resume conversations with patients who hadn't decided what they wanted to do. This was happening almost every day.

A friend was debating whether to get the vaccine. He was told it was made in China and wasn't sure he should take it. I explained that the benefits of the vaccine likely outweighed the risks. In the end, he decided to get vaccinated.

But stories beat science, every time. They were much more effective than explaining the science. When I told resistant patients about a patient who died recently, whose mother kept telling me, through her tears, that she wished her son had gotten vaccinated, their resistance often broke down.

A friend asked me: "Is it true that if someone has both diabetes and COVID-19 but dies from diabetes, the medical people are calling it a COVID-19 death so they can do more treatments and make more money?"

I explained that if someone has diabetes and COVID-19, and their lungs fail because of COVID-19, we record it as a COVID-19 death, although their comorbidities might be listed as well.

The most troubling questions were the ones left unasked. They added a layer of complexity to the conversation that made me feel bad for both the doctors and patients. The distrust became visceral.

When I was in Montana during a COVID-19 surge, one of my patients delivered a long, animated rant about how much he hated Chinese people. I was gowned up with my face masked, so he couldn't tell I was Asian.

"It's the Chinese! The Chinese people brought this upon us!"

The nurse looked at me with a mixture of concern and amusement, while I tried my best not to laugh out loud from behind my headgear.

It's hard for patients who don't trust doctors. It's just as hard for doctors when their patients don't trust them. It's sad to think that someone who's had a primary care physician for twenty years could lose trust in that doctor after watching a few videos on social media.

We don't have that problem of trust when we're on medical relief missions. Our international patients trust us completely—maybe too much.

On one mission in Myanmar a woman came to the clinic with a large thyroid mass that was likely cancerous. I explained that it would be very risky to remove it with the limited capacity we had.

"I'm willing to accept the risk," she said. "If something goes wrong, then I trust that you did your best."

I removed the cancer, but she lost her voice because of nerve injury on one side. I felt horrible. She was a teacher and wouldn't be able to talk because of me. Nevertheless, she maintained a positive attitude. When we returned the next year, I was relieved to discover that she had recovered much of her voice, yet I still felt guilty. Even if you did the best you could, you feel you failed the patient.

The pandemic has heightened this sense of responsibility among health care workers. We wanted to do everything we could but were often overwhelmed by the numbers of patients we had, while the hospitals were constantly complaining that we weren't doing enough. Families were angry with us, and patients were refusing treatment out of mistrust.

I had a patient in the ICU named David who needed a permanent pacemaker. His cardiologist had explained to him that without the procedure he was going to keep having fatal heart rhythms and die. David didn't want the procedure and refused to see the cardiologist again.

I walked into the room to find him in his bed, looking disgruntled. I sat down and asked him how he was feeling. "Not great, obviously," he said. "But I'm not gonna let you kill me by putting that thing in my chest."

I explained that there was a risk to the procedure, but he was kept alive with a temporary pacemaker that he couldn't go home with.

"I don't need it!" David cried, scratching his wild beard and refusing to meet my eyes. "I'm a good man, and I trust that things will happen the way they should. Let God decide."

I tried to explain to him that his heart wasn't working well enough to keep him alive without the pacemaker.

"You think I'm dumb?" he said. "You're telling me what the cardiologist said!"

"We're trying to help you have the best chance of living," I told him.

"I know the government sent you to implant a tracking device in me," he muttered.

He was really sick and on medications, so it was possible he was hallucinating. He was so angry and upset that he wouldn't talk to his family.

I called his daughter.

"That's strange; he's not usually like this."

She tried to call him, but he didn't answer. She wanted to convince him to agree to the procedure, but she couldn't come in and speak with him in person during the height of the pandemic.

I returned to his room and sat down next to his bed.

"Look," I said. "You do whatever you want, but can I tell you a story?"

He gave me a suspicious look, then told me to go ahead.

When there are no logical arguments that will convince a patient, I resort to telling a classic story about faith and adjust it to fit the situation.

"I met another patient with a heart problem last year. The surgeon told him he needed a procedure, but the patient refused, saying that God would make him better. The cardiologist then told the man he needed a defibrillator, but he insisted that God would take care of him.

"I came in and I said, 'I think you should listen to the cardiologist.' And he said, 'I trust that God will save me.' An hour after he went home, this man went into cardiac arrest. The paramedics arrived minutes later and did everything they could, but he died."

David listened intently.

"If he went to heaven and asked God why he didn't save him, God might have told him, 'I tried to save you—I sent a surgeon, a cardiologist, and an ICU doctor to help you, but you turned them all away.'"

"I like that story," said David.

The next day he called back the cardiologist and got his pacemaker.

Our daily jobs are stressful, and most health care workers are undervalued and overworked, but it's the bureaucracy that pushes many of us to leave medicine. A doctor friend of mine told me she's not able to effectively do her job because of all the red tape. The administrative burden contributes to our moral defeat.

Since I've become a doctor, I've seen the medical system become more bureaucratic and over-regulated. The administrator-to-doctor ratio has skyrocketed, while the number of actual doctors has only slightly increased. Currently, there are as many as a dozen administrators for every doctor on staff. The business side of medicine can be out of touch with what doctors and nurses do. Good intentions are not enough— we need to be better aligned.

Many of the metrics we're expected to meet interfere with our ability to do our jobs effectively. For example, at one facility we have to meet a smoking cessation metric. If we don't talk about the harms of smoking with 80 percent of our patients, we don't pass the metric. This makes no sense for a trauma surgeon. When a patient comes in with a gunshot wound, the conversation is not going to be about quitting smoking.

I could say, "I need you to stop smoking" and check off the metric. But I would feel dishonest if I did that, so I don't meet that metric.

Patient evaluations play a large role in how doctors are rated, which can create harm. If a patient requests a medication that a doctor feels is unnecessary, the doctor may prescribe it anyway to avoid a negative evaluation. Doctors should make decisions based on what is medically best for patients, not on what will make them happy.

Furthermore, surgeons who do complex or emergency procedures are more likely to have more negative outcomes or complications, yet this isn't taken into account when measuring their ratings. An emergency surgery presents far more risks for the patient than an elective procedure, but both are evaluated using the same standards.

This administrative burden is preventing many doctors from delivering optimum health care to their patients. It seems that everywhere you look there are numbers and spreadsheets, and the driving force behind health care decisions is no longer oath or compassion but accountants and the bottom line.

I understand the need to meet financial goals. But I also know that if we deliver good health care, the bottom line will be fine. If we start out putting profit first, the result will be compromised health care.

When we're required to use certain equipment because it's cheaper, it takes longer to do procedures and causes more complications. That's not good for anyone—not the patients, the doctors, or the bottom line. But someone, somewhere, decided to pay more attention to profit than to people.

Many of the leaders only stay in their positions for a few years, so they're not motivated to make changes that could make their jobs harder. They would rather not rock the boat and just maintain the status quo.

The health care system was broken before COVID-19 hit. The pandemic merely magnified the greed and dysfunction that was already present. I had hoped that these issues would come under scrutiny during the pandemic, but while the problems are more apparent than ever, they are still not being addressed.

I've seen nurses burnt out to the point of tears on their shifts. I remember seeing a thirty-five-year-old nurse retire because she couldn't take the stress anymore. One nurse told me he was going to quit and open an Etsy shop. Sometimes I think about leaving medicine to pursue another passion, like painting. But most days I can't imagine not being a doctor.

A gastroenterologist friend of mine passed out while doing laundry and was admitted to the hospital. We thought she had suffered a stroke, but her tests were negative. She had just collapsed from exhaustion.

A cardiologist I work with was so tired that he tripped when leaving the hospital and broke his wrist. He'd been working at least twenty hours straight. Despite his injury, he had to go right back to work the next day. His wrist took months to heal.

We've experienced a mental health pandemic hand in hand with COVID-19. Divorces are up among doctors and nurses. Everyone's on edge. And more health care professionals are taking their lives.

Very few have been writing and talking about the forbidden topic of physician suicide. Doctors kill themselves at a rate more than twice that of the general population, which puts them near the top of the list of professions with the highest suicide rate— and this was before COVID-19. This fact is largely swept under the rug. Doctors tend not to ask for help. Health care workers who publicly discuss these issues are often criticized, but many others feel these discussions must be had.

If we're putting in a hundred hours a week, constantly surrounded by our patients' pain, we have no time left to deal with our own health, and the result is dysfunction in our personal lives.

After working long hours under immense pressure, some doctors find it difficult to cope once the pressure is off. I knew an ICU doctor who was always picking up extra shifts to help out. When he took an extended vacation, he found that he became suicidal. He eventually killed himself.

A year into the COVID-19 pandemic, an ER doctor in Hawaii killed himself. He was playful and jovial, and worked constantly during the pandemic. A friend of the ER doc wrote: "He died a few hours after we had dinner. He shared the pain of watching COVID-19 patients die. I told him it must be hard. *Yes*, he replied, *but it's my job*. The last thing he told me was how hard it was to talk to a patient about the likelihood of survival after going on a ventilator. He knew survival wasn't very likely, but he didn't want to be brutally honest with them either. Again he said, *That's my job*. My friend was known as the ER doctor with the sense of humor, who kept everyone happy during the worst times. He liked posting memes and jokes, especially dirty or irreverent ones. He loved wearing silly costumes and wigs."

A memo circulated throughout the hospital to acknowledge his passing but with no mention of the suicide. Everyone who worked with him knew how he died; the hospital refused to talk about it. Suicide among doctors is a taboo subject. Who wants to be a patient at a hospital where the doctors are killing themselves?

Our hospital chaplain was supposed to moderate a group therapy session over Zoom, but it was canceled by administration. It had been hard to convince ten health care workers to sign up for therapy, so we were disappointed. The hospital may have canceled the therapy session because of liability issues or because they thought a psychologist should run it instead of a chaplain.

But all was not lost. A psychologist outside the hospital system volunteered to do mental health counseling. We started with an inaugural group of six women. All of us were experiencing stressors that were exacerbated during the pandemic. We met weekly for two years, and during that time we became a lot more effective in our jobs. We are all still in touch and continue to support each other.

According to a psychiatrist who spoke at a conference, while nurses frequently ask for help, doctors rarely do. Some do try to seek counseling without anyone knowing for fear of jeopardizing their careers.

The reticence is due to deep shame, the psychiatrist said. Doctors don't think of their profession as a job. Rather, it's their identity. It's who you are. If doctors are failing on the job, they believe they're failing at life.

The intense stresses brought about by COVID-19 have made it more acceptable to ask for help. There's a greater understanding of the emotional damage caused by moral injury.

When I started my surgery residency, we were told that four residents and staff had killed themselves in recent years, and I think my program was typical. I looked around at my peers and thought, *I hope none of you do that*. I had that worry in the back of my mind all through residency. Suicide in the profession wasn't on my radar before I became a doctor, but knowing about it wouldn't have deterred me from becoming one.

Chapter Twelve
The Way It Could Be

We behave as if health care is an unlimited resource, and that is a dangerous assumption to make.

We're seeing a disturbing trend of people dying from heart disease, advanced cancers, asthma/COPD exacerbations, and stroke because hospitals are overwhelmed and can't provide adequate care. This is especially apparent in our current morbidity and mortality rates, which are appalling despite our enormous health care spending.

When we were providing disaster relief in COVID ICUs during the pandemic, I recognized clear similarities with our deployments in Haiti, South Sudan, and the Syrian border. Parts of the mainland US were behaving like developing nations, with hospitals filled beyond capacity, limited resources, and burned-out health care workers.

In Hawaii we considered using ECMO to treat COVID-19 patients with respiratory failure who had not responded to conventional management. ECMO, or extracorporeal membrane oxygenation, is a last-resort mechanical system that supports the circulation and gas exchange of patients whose hearts or lungs are failing. The machine does the work of the heart and lungs when they can't do it well enough themselves.

ECMO is very resource intensive, requiring a team of highly trained specialists and a lot of expensive equipment. Nevertheless, it's a promising treatment for COVID-19 patients with respiratory failure and can save lives, and we wanted to make sure it was available to as many people as possible.

Yet the pandemic has created a new level of inequality in the US, with those who have access to the best medical care (ECMO machines and providers) having a much better chance of survival than those who don't. The US medical system is looking more and more like that of developing nations, often lacking the resources and personnel needed to save lives.

During the pandemic, hospitals were struggling to communicate with each other about which patients were most in need of treatment. Decisions about when to use certain limited resources were being made without a clear plan or process. This created a situation where some patients were receiving the care they needed while others were being left behind. We needed to work together to see the big picture, so we could make sure that everyone was receiving the best possible care.

A colleague therefore started a grassroots group to share information quickly and efficiently about COVID-19 patients among all the intensivist groups in Hawaii. Standard regulations and processes that had been designed for normal operation were not sufficient for surge communication during a pandemic. The grassroots group quickly became a lifeline for sharing critical information among intensivists and helped to keep more patients alive.

Health care shortages are a global problem, and in some places the problem is more acute than others. We're not used to such shortages in the US.

At several of the hospitals where I work, we often struggle to find surgeons who are willing to be on call. This means that the same surgeons often have to work several days in a row, for very long hours.

A man came to the emergency room complaining of severe abdominal pain from a hole in his stomach caused by an ulcer. Everyone was scrambling to find a surgeon to operate on this patient. The surgeon on call was operating at another hospital.

The ER doctor asked me, "If we can't find a surgeon, would you take this patient?"

"I can't leave the ICU," I said. "But we'll figure something out."

The patient was getting sicker by the minute, his stomach juices leaking out. If we couldn't find a surgeon to take the patient immediately, my intensivist partner was ready to stay after his night shift to cover my ICU patients for a few hours to enable me to do the surgery. At the last minute we did get ahold of a surgeon, who canceled his morning clinic to do the operation.

The patient was brought to the operating room for an exploratory laparotomy. I scrubbed in for a bit before going back to the ICU. We found his belly full of bile from a one-centimeter hole in the stomach. I went back to the ICU while the surgeon plugged the hole with a piece of omentum, then sutured the plug in place. He then irrigated the abdomen and closed the patient. The patient was back in his ICU room in less than two hours and out of the ICU the next day. He was lucky we were able to find a surgeon.

Some industry leaders are motivated primarily by money. They prioritize short-term financial gain over the success of the organization. While I'd like to believe that most medical leaders care about our patients, it isn't always the case.

Even the most well-intentioned health care leaders may not always offer the best solutions. They may find their hospitals struggling and respond by hiring more employees or purchasing more equipment. But sometimes the solution is more nuanced than that. More of the same isn't always helpful.

If a surgeon had been on call specifically for emergency general surgery, the patient with the stomach ulcer would have been taken to the operating room sooner and might not have needed to spend a day in the ICU. Having the right number of surgeons in the right places can save lives.

Some problems have obvious solutions, but people, organizations, and cultures are not easy to change.

Years ago, primary care physicians (PCPs) would visit their patients in hospitals to provide care. However, today's PCPs are too busy to do so. Instead, hospitalized patients are now taken care of by hospitalists. This is generally a more efficient way of doing things, as these doctors are in the hospital twenty-four-seven.

We used to have general surgeons who were like PCPs. They would take care of lumps and bumps in their clinics, then perform scheduled surgeries in hospitals. Today's busy general surgeon does not have time to be on call while she's seeing patients in the clinic or doing scheduled elective surgeries like colon resections, hernia repairs, or gastric bypasses.

When she's in the operating room, the emergency room physician might call about a car crash victim with a ruptured spleen. To save the patient in the ER, the surgeon may need to cancel the next surgery or delay clinic.

Now, as we have hospitalists as the inpatient counterparts to PCPs, we also have acute care surgeons who partner with clinic-based general surgeons. We're trained in the same ways but serve different functions.

I'm an acute care surgeon. I take on unscheduled emergency surgeries and help other surgeons with difficult surgeries. When a patient shows up in the ER with a ruptured appendix and I happen to be on call, I won't need to cancel elective surgeries or delay clinic. I don't have regular office hours or scheduled surgeries. Because I'm not doing multiple, conflicting things simultaneously, it's a more efficient approach both for the patient and the hospital.

Each hospital system is unique, so what works for one system may not apply to another. At many large hospital systems, there are advantages (medical and financial) to having an acute care surgery service.

We've been advocating for acute care surgeons as a solution to more efficient patient care, but while some hospitals are doing it and doing it well, this change is happening too slowly to the frustration of some of my surgery colleagues.

Finance departments need several years of data to compare one system of operations to another. One problem is that the metrics being used to measure cost versus savings don't always consider true costs.

For example, when patients are taken care of sooner, they are less sick, require fewer resources, go home sooner, and have less extensive future medical needs. Patients don't have to wait as long for surgery. Adding acute care surgeons can help improve surgical efficiency and patient outcomes. And when elective general surgeons take fewer days of call, they're able to spend more time doing elective cases. But these efficiencies are often not considered in making the decision to add acute care surgeons.

Separating acute care surgery from elective general surgery is a concept that doesn't make sense everywhere. In rural hospitals the same surgeons can provide elective as well as emergency surgical care. My hospital system is open to having an acute care surgery service, but the concept is taking some time for them to digest.

As we make the right changes, the hospital will run more smoothly, patient length of stay will shorten, the bottom line will improve, and the community will be healthier.

The international missions and my work in the US are interrelated. In both, we need to move health care in a direction that makes sense for patients, and we need to live up to the dictum "first, do no harm." Both at home and abroad, it's not enough to simply see patients with diabetes, heart disease, or hypertension and give them medicine. We need to do more to help them manage their conditions and improve their overall health.

Many people believe that the main purpose of international aid missions is for patients to be seen by American doctors or to undergo procedures that only we can perform. This shouldn't be the case. The goal of our missions should be to make ourselves obsolete, to support countries in becoming self-sustaining after we leave, and to put an end to crises so that they don't linger indefinitely. Even though this is unlikely to happen in my lifetime, it is something to strive for. If there is a shortage of surgeons in the United States, it is highly unlikely that there will be enough surgeons in Myanmar or South Sudan.

Crisis care is what many aid groups do best. When somebody is shot, we bandage them up. But once the crisis is over, many groups pretend that there is still a crisis or invent a new one. They keep showing up long after they are needed.

On one mission in Haiti, we weren't very organized. We met up with another NGO to see if we could collaborate. They started a mobile clinic and we helped them manage it. We'd show up to a village and treat what was, for the most part, a healthy population. Two months later, another aid group would show up and treat them again.

When a patient has an active infection, it's helpful to have an antibiotic to treat it. However, if someone has a chronic complaint, I don't see how an aid group that shows up for two weeks can be of much help.

I traveled to several countries to provide COVID-19 response. It was strange being part of a US aid team overseas when we were the ones who needed the help, not them. But we did our best to share our knowledge and experience with our foreign counterparts, in the hope that they could learn from our mistakes. We made the best of it, but much of what we did could have been done online. It felt more like a PR exercise than a medical one. I couldn't help but wonder why we were even there.

I also wonder about the entire concept of international aid when our own country is facing so many crises. Near the end of writing this book, a patient enraged about pain from his back surgery killed two doctors, a receptionist, and a patient at a trauma hospital in Tulsa, Oklahoma, where I used to work. Two days before that someone shot four people at a park a few blocks from our hospital in downtown Honolulu. A nurse at our hospital was walking her dog and a bullet grazed her leg.

After one of my night shifts I had breakfast with a doctor who works in addiction treatment. We talked about how it's nearly impossible to kick certain addictions, like methamphetamine, which causes an incredible dopamine release. Our brains aren't designed to produce that much dopamine. Hawaii, which appears on the surface to be a paradise, has a huge meth problem that's becoming increasingly hard to ignore.

Meth is scary. I see the drug's effects every day in my line of work. People become quickly addicted and spiral out of control. Some patients with "meth hearts" don't make it out alive. Of those who do, many continue to use. I don't know how to fix the meth problem, but I know it will take a team of people to make that possible.

When I think of what makes medical care successful and gratifying, either at home or around the world, it always comes back to the team I work with.

On a mission in Myanmar, our team was working smoothly, in sync. We were able to do more procedures in a day because we didn't have to deal with the regulatory disruption that happens so often at home. I was able to work as a doctor, not as a representative of the medical enterprise. On some international missions there are sometimes four or five of us operating at the same time in one room, which does not happen in the States.

At the hospital in Hawaii where I work, one of the surgeons was doing a difficult case. She asked if I could help her because it was a two-surgeon job. The operation was on a tumor that was abutting the inferior vena cava, a very dangerous area.

An orthopedic spine surgeon poked his head in our operating room and saw that we were carefully dissecting out the mass. He wanted to take a look, since we were working near the spine, and then left. It was his way of letting us know that if we needed his help, he was around. A vascular surgeon came in to check out the dissection, and then another general surgeon dropped in to say hi. Their way of letting us know we had backup if we needed it.

I've found that the key to good medicine is teamwork. If the team dynamic isn't good, or if the surgeons and nurses don't get along, I'm not going to stick around and try to fix the system. I've worked in hospitals where I liked most of the people, but the team wasn't cohesive enough for me to stay.

At my current hospital, I have the family and teamwork that I need. It's helpful if at least some of the people on the team are also trying to improve the system. Not everyone needs to be a reformer, but it's important that there are some good people in the right places who are willing to listen and make improvements.

What's frustrating is that the administrators will change every few years. My hope is there are enough good people in the right places who are willing to stay, listen, and make improvements. Only then will we have the health care system we need and deserve.

Epilogue
Dear Mom

Y ou died on your fifty-third birthday. From time to time, I imagine what you would be like today had you lived. How would you have changed? Would I have developed a better understanding of you, of our relationship, of who you were? And you of me?

We rarely saw each other during the seven years before you died, so you're frozen in time. I can sometimes hear you speaking to me, as the person you were then. *Oh Cecily, I was right after all. I told you not to go to med school. You didn't listen to me, and now look at you—working crazy hours instead of relaxing in a comfortable home and enjoying life. You don't have a husband, you don't have children, you don't even have a house!*

It may be pure fantasy on my part, but if you were alive today at seventy-five, I hope you would be able to say to me, "I don't know why you want this kind of life, traveling to all these poor countries, working all these crazy hours, but it's fine with me. I'm happy for you because you're doing exactly what you're supposed to be doing."

Perhaps it is pure fantasy, after all.

Sometimes when I'm on a deployment overseas, I'll talk to you, composing a letter in my head that can't be sent.

Dear Mom,

It's been twenty-three years since you died. I'm not sure whether you're still around in some form, or if you can see what's going on in the world these days, but I thought you'd enjoy a brief (albeit overdue) update…

Family:

Your funeral was beautiful. Everyone was there. Lots of crying and laughing. Afterward, Rocky and I decided to get matching tattoos—half of a king snake on our right hands, so when we put them together it makes a whole.

The tattoo on my left forearm has changed from the one you might remember. I had it redone around ten years ago.

Your siblings still fight about dumb things. Rocky and I are still good friends. He makes some of your dishes, like your potato salad, when he visits. Dad married Lydia. She's nice and probably good for him. They're both hoarders. They have two houses full of things they don't need or use. Some have memories for Dad (so I guess he does need them). Rocky intermittently helps him organize and downsize. I'm too impatient to help. It's no big deal; we don't really talk about the piles of boxes anymore.

Me:

I did end up going to medical school, against your advice. All your worries about me were real; it took me ten years to become a surgeon, and another year of fellowship to become an ICU doctor. During those eleven years, the only week I traveled was to Haiti in 2006. The other weeks were eighty-plus hours of working/training in hospitals with the rest of the time spent studying at home. The thing is, I enjoyed the long days/months/years of surgeon and intensivist training. The hours didn't drag. I often stayed later than needed so I could "squeeze in" some time in the operating room or the ICU. Most people (including you, Rocky, and Dad) would have hated this ridiculous life and schedule. But I loved my time in "doctor boot camp."

Now my work involves a combination of surgery, ICU work, medical missions (helping in other countries after earthquakes, floods, wars, etc.), and teaching medical students and residents. I do paint, but I'm a better doctor than an artist, probably because of all the training.

I'm neither married nor in a serious partnership. These things aren't important to me.

You and me:

We were so unlike one another. As a child and young adult, I had trouble wrapping my head around why I was okay with our differences, but you were not. I now understand that you, like many people (but not me), preferred to be around people with similar views. It must have been so disturbing to have a child you loved who didn't see eye to eye with you on so many levels.

If you were physically here today, I'm pretty sure we'd get along fine. With time, I bet our clashing personalities would have found ways to make peace. By now I've learned to connect with almost everyone. Some of my favorite people remind me of you.

If my thoughts and words still don't make sense to you, it's okay. We don't have to make sense to each other anymore, right?

The world:

I look for the people who can make the changes we need. I hope there are enough effective "disruptors" out there to turn things around for us. Some days I believe there's hope for humanity. When I don't, I meditate and try to live in the moment.

Despite all the problems in the world, I'm happy most of the time. I default to the things that matter:

connections, art, laughter, reducing pain and suffering, learning, breathing, good food.

I've thought from time to time about how my career has been devoted to helping people who've suffered unfairness or injustice regain control and harmony in their disrupted lives. Lives disrupted by arbitrary forces, by luck and happenstance, divorced from any understandable reasons or causes. Maybe I want to see people regain the kind of harmony and control that didn't exist in our relationship. Maybe my missions are, in some ways, my attempt to redo our past.

But mostly I do missions because I need to. Doctoring feels like an obligation, not a choice or a burden. I like being where I'm needed most. The people I work with on missions are my family. I come back home a better surgeon and a better person.

All you wanted was for me to be happy, comfortable, and taken care of. I wanted more. I wanted to be useful, needed, helpful.

I've learned that I don't need to "accept the things I cannot change." Instead, I recognize those things that I can't change and accept that I can't change them. There's a subtle but important difference. I can't change those parts of our relationship that were painful and damaging for me. But that doesn't mean I accept what happened between us. I can forgive you, while not accepting that part of our shared past.

I can't change the poverty and injustice I see in our country and around the world, but I don't accept that nothing can be done about them. I do what I can to change what's possible, to heal the wounds that can be healed, to help those who can be helped. And I accept those times when it wasn't possible, when the decisions I made were flawed, when the demands were far beyond what I had to work with in the moment. I keep my focus not on all those who need care, but on who and what is right in front of me. I'll always be a doctor because that's who I am.

I did the harder thing, took the harder path, and that made me a better person. It forced me to grow in ways I couldn't have imagined when I first took this path. My work has stretched me beyond my limits, forced me to make painful sacrifices, and exposed me to the worst in human nature.

But, far more often, it has shown me the very best in humanity.

Mom, I hope you're happy too.

All my love,

Cecily

About the Author

Cecily Wang is a trauma surgeon and intensive care physician in Hawaii. She was born in Taipei, Taiwan, and immigrated to the US with her family when she was eight years old. Dr. Wang has extensive medical training in general surgery and trauma critical care medicine. She has served both domestically and internationally as a member of Médecins Sans Frontières (Doctors Without Borders) and several other aid groups. Cecily believes a positive impact can be made by a small group of caring individuals, and she loves getting her patients to laugh, even if it hurts their incisions a bit. In addition to medical relief work, she enjoys traveling and creating art.

9 781662 936852